TITIAN

TITIAN

Text by Antonio Morassi

New York Graphic Society

Greenwich, Connecticut

Library of Congress Catalog Number 65-23598

Literary and reproduction rights reserved for all countries

© 1964 by "Silvana" Editoriale D'Arte - Milan - Italy

Printed in Italy

Fig. 1. *Sleeping Venus*. Dresden, Gallery.

I

Titian has always been considered one of the greatest painters who ever lived. He ranks as an equal with his contemporaries Leonardo, Raphael, Giorgione, and Michelangelo, especially the latter with whom he shares both majestic vision and conceptual force. His art belongs to a new world that is still alive in our times, for in transcending Renaissance ideals, he opened new horizons in painting to artists such as Velazquez, Rubens, and Rembrandt. European painting since the 16th century would be inconceivable without the achievements of Titian. His greatness was recognized in Venice during his lifetime; next to Giorgione he appears as a new star lighting the entire century of art. Outside Venice his fame spread rapidly to the courts of Europe, culminating in papal recognition and appointment as court painter to Charles V and later to Philip II. When Charles V, Emperor of the Holy Roman Empire, chose him as court painter, it was tantamount to being recognized as the supreme, living authority in art.

Are the criteria of Titian's contemporaries and critics still valid today? Naturally, the question involves the larger problem of the extent to which an artist can be understood by critics of his own time. In the history of art, many an artist has not been fully understood. True, this has occurred more frequently in the recent past, especially in the late 19th century, when, indeed, a real upheaval of artistic and spiritual values occurred along the lines of Nietzsche's " Umwertung aller Werte " — (re-evaluation of all values). In the past, instances of misunderstanding the artist were very rare; they were confined primarily to what may be called the " old-age " styles of the artist, namely, the late periods of Michelangelo and Rembrandt or, for that matter, Beethoven and Goethe.

Titian was considered a sublime artist during his lifetime because he fully embodied the ideals to which the great men of his time aspired. This has always been true of great masters, whether it be Phidias or Giotto, Tiepolo or Goya. The rupture between the artist and his public (meaning people who are knowledgeable about art) occurred when artists expressed ideas that exceeded the receptive capacity of their audience. This happened, probably for the first time in the history of painting, to the late works of Titian.

The first pictures of the young Titian seem to have provoked great excitement among the Venetians. According to Dolce, who writes about the earliest fresco decoration for the Fondaco dei Tedeschi in 1508 by Titian and his master Giorgione, so great was Titian's success that Giorgione is said to have closed himself up at home, depressed and humiliated. So grand was Titian's artistic development during the decade after these frescoes that his painting of the *Assumption* for the Church of the Frari in 1518 was acclaimed something of a miracle. From that moment on, Titian continued to produce masterpieces which made him the undisputed master of Venetian and European painting, anticipating its aspirations and embodying the loftiest ideals of the era.

As Titian's style changed and developed, at last becoming intensely introspective and fantastic once tradition was broken and a new freedom was found, the opinion of his contemporaries began to waver. The more Titian advanced in years, the less his paintings were understood. The works of his old age — the very paintings which seem to us to represent the most sublime expression of his genius — were criticized as weak and lacking in form. Michelangelo's alleged criticism of Titian's imperfect draftsmanship as related by Vasari (incidentally, one of Titian's greatest admirers) seems symptomatic of contemporary opinion. It is doubtful, however, that Michelangelo ever made such a statement since Titian was in Rome in 1545 when his draftsmanship left nothing to be desired; it is more likely that the remark reflects Vasari's own opinion, attributable to his own reluctance to praise the Venetian painter over the " divine " Florentine, Michelangelo. Our doubts seem justified when we note that in Michelangelo's " unfinished " late style of form there is the same mystical, poetic feeling as in the unfinished forms of Titian's " old-age " style.

Titian's precociousness as a youth was sustained and developed progressively as he strove to reassess his art and to express ever more mystic and profound ideas. Throughout his old age until his death in 1576, his painting continued to mature, not merely in terms of livelier color, the full range of which he had already achieved in his youth, but in a widening of the function of color. Color assumes a life of its own, free from form and creating its own form, independent of drawing and totally free to pursue its own course.

In Titian's late style, color became the vehicle for transfiguring and transcendent effects. Among his contemporaries, and except for Tintoretto, the only one of his students who fully understood his use of color was Domenico Theotocopuli, called El Greco. El

6

Fig. 2. *Madonna and Child with Saints Roch and Anthony.* Madrid, Prado.

Greco's art develops out of Titian's pictorial premises, although its great expressiveness occurred after Titian's death when he had settled in Spain at the turn of the century. Other great painters of the 17th century came under Titian's influence. We think immediately of Velazquez, whose ineffable play of color variants and gentle strokes of a seemingly hairless brush in passages of supreme delicacy achieved his extraordinarily refined color effects, and Rembrandt, whose thick impasto of color and the ease of his brushstroke in his more mature works enabled him to achieve a form of expression unprecedented in Dutch painting, and best suited to his visions of tragedy and loneliness. To these artists we may add Rubens, van Dyck, and Frans Hals, to mention only the greatest.

Why trace later reflections of Titian's art? Sensitive artists have always been stimulated by it. Fra Galgario of Bergamo, one of the best portraitists of the 18th century, kept a painting by Titian as inspiration for his own work which became increasingly richer in mysterious tones. His biographer, Tassi, states that in his last years he emulated Titian by applying color with his fingers rather than with a brush. Fra Galgario was an isolated example in a century which worshipped Paolo Veronese for his gay silvery colors and rich figure compositions. The 18th century looked at some of Tintoretto's dynamic canvases only when the need for a more dramatic accent was felt. It accepted, though not enthusiastically, the paintings of Titian's youth and maturity, admiring the lyricism and the classical beauty of his early paintings of Venus. Titian's late paintings were

Fig. 3. *Sacred Conversation of Casa Balbi.* Genoa, Palazzo Balbi-Piovera.

ignored completely. And during the Neo-classical period, these works naturally were all but forgotten.

Only toward the end of the 19th century, when new directions in painting had been taken by Delacroix, Manet, and Cézanne, is there a re-evaluation of Titian's late works. Delacroix, in particular, was the first of the 19th century artists who understood Titian's œuvre in its entirety, a fact that is evident in the influence it had on his own painting and in notes about Titian recorded in his diary: " If one lived to be a hundred and twenty years old, one would prefer Titian to all else. He is not the man for young people. He is the least mannered, consequently the most varied of painters " (*Journal*, 1857; translation by Walter Pach). Turning to the observations of art historians, Cavalcaselle's outstanding monograph (1871) contains passages revealing at least his partial awareness of the significant meaning of Titian's late paintings. Early in the 20th century, when El Greco was being discovered, there was a new interest in Titian's late style. To illustrate the lack of comprehension in Titian's late works, we may mention that a masterpiece like *Tarquinius and Lucrezia* (Plate 38), acquired by the Vienna Academy only in 1907, had to be withdrawn from display because of the great scandal it provoked. Yet a few years later, after it had been published by Bode, it was once again exhibited to admiring connoisseurs.

8

The strange destiny of Titian's late works was paralleled in another way by the fate of his youthful paintings. They appeared so miraculously beautiful that it seemed impossible that Titian, not his master Giorgione, could have painted them. Titian found himself dispossessed, so to speak, of his early works through public opinion and the notions of some contemporary writers even during his lifetime. The elegiac mood of the landscape in these early works and their mood of reverie still reflected the mystic charm first introduced into painting by Giorgione. Indeed, the controversy over the attributions of the works to Giorgione rather than to his pupil Titian has persisted almost into our days; among some scholars, right to the present. Thus, the persistent lack of understanding of Titian's late works did — in an inverse sense — affect also the masterpieces of his youth, making the rediscovery of the young Titian another gratifying achievement of recent studies in art history.

The controversy over attributions began in Titian's lifetime and increased with the spread of the Giorgione myth which began immediately after his untimely death. Vasari attributed the *Christ and the Rascal* in the Church of San Roch to Giorgione in the first edition (1550) of his *Lives,* and to Titian in the second edition of 1568 — proof of the undecided authorship even then of a work which I believe to be entirely by the hand of Titian. The attributions of many other masterpieces have long been debated: the *Knight of Malta* (Pitti Gallery); the *Fête Champêtre* (Louvre); the *Concert* (Pitti Gallery); the

Fig. 4. So-called *Portrait of Ariosto*. London, National Gallery.

Fig. 5. *Noli me tangere*. London, National Gallery.

9

Fig. 6. *Portrait of a Young Man.* London, Earl of Halifax Collection.   Fig. 7. *Man in a Red Cap.* New York, Frick Collection.

Adulteress (Glasgow); the *Noli me tangere* (National Gallery, London); the *Madonna and two Saints* (Prado). These are among the major works now reattributed almost unanimously to the young Titian, while the still disputed *Sleeping Venus* (Dresden) seems to me to be a work of Titian's early period.

An unusual early period this must have been, since according to Dolce (1557) Titian's own teacher, Giorgione, emphasized his miraculous precocity in stating that, " he was a painter even in his mother's womb. " Truly, an extraordinary genius.

Few artists have equalled Titian's vast creative range, and in even fewer is there such a profound difference between their early and late works. Rembrandt comes to mind; in his early phase, a meticulous realist, in his old age an artist who transformed reality into a new poetry of chiaroscuro. One thinks also of the differences that mark Beethoven's early, Mozartean symphonies from his late, mystical quartets, or the early and the late Verdi. Similarly, there is a world of difference between the *Sacred and Profane Love* painted by Titian when he was about twenty-five years old and the unfinished *Pieta* in Venice, a work of his last years. It may be argued that considering Titian's long life a gradual change of style and conceptions was unavoidable. Even so, his creative process, always alive, shows an impressive range of ideas. However, Titian did not live to be a centenarian, as was long believed on the basis of old but unconfirmed assertions regarding his exceptional longevity. Titian's alleged and much cited lifetime of a hundred years, which contributed no little to his fame, is part of the myth surrounding the artist which for practical reasons he himself promoted. Actually, Titian died when he was about

10

ninety, judging from the statements of Dolce (1557) and Vasari (1568). The fact that he worked indefatigably until his last days, even creating some of his greatest masterpieces as a very old man, is extraordinary and almost unique in the history of art.

* * *

Titian was born at Pieve di Cadore, probably ca. 1488-90, the descendant of an old family whose origins go back to the 13th century. The family name derives from one Guacello or Vecellio, mayor of Cadore in the first half of the 14th century. The name of Titian's father was Gregorio, whose wife bore him five sons, one of them our artist. Little is known about Titian's first teachers. According to Dolce, he was sent at the age of nine to an uncle in Venice who placed him in the workshop of Sebastiano Zuccato. This was the father of the renowned mosaicists Valerio and Francesco who became Titian's friends and whose double portrait he painted.

This early apprenticeship is not devoid of importance if we assume that his technique of color separation has some affinity with mosaic art. In any event, the young painter soon left Zuccato to work first in the shop of Gentile Bellini and later in that of Giovanni Bellini. Not long afterwards Titian seems to have been attracted by the new style of Giorgione in whom he found his ideal master. This is the traditional theory which has been largely confirmed. A friend, more than a mere teacher, Giorgione soon entrusted to Titian part of the frescoes on the Fondaco dei Tedeschi which he executed in 1508.

The influence of the Bellinis on the young Titian is relatively slight. It amounts to little more than the general composition of the altarpiece now in Antwerp (erroneously dated 1503 by some scholars, when it should be a decade later), and the archaic Bellinesque elements in paintings such as *The Gypsy* and the *Madonna with the Cherries*, both in Vienna, and the *Virgin with Saints Roch and Anthony* (Prado). In these first works of Titian there is much greater power, freedom and spontaneity of execution. I would say that what is Bellinesque about the paintings is their flavor, their tonality, and the touch of homeliness. Beyond this point in Titian's work there is nothing of the Bellinis.

The question of Giorgione's influence on the other hand is much more complex and admittedly harder to distinguish. Recently, a question has been raised whether Titian learned the fundamentals of painting from Giorgione. If he did not, where else could his art have originated? To me the basis of Titian's artistic origins in Giorgione's art is incontrovertible. To mention only essential elements, there is in the young Titian's work the lyrical sentiment and spiritual atmosphere of Giorgione, so much so that Titian's earliest paintings were mistaken for Giorgione's, and some still are today. There is also his powerful sense of color, inherited directly from Giorgione. Indeed, in contrast with the painting techniques of Giovanni Bellini, the more progressive of the Bellinis, Giorgione's new style was revolutionary. In Giorgione's mature works may be seen the broken-color technique, (criticized by Vasari for its " inattention to drawing ") which Titian later developed to such perfection. Titian seems to me to be Giorgione's artistic descendant, endowed with even greater imagination and a brilliant vision. Not for nothing is the distinction between Giorgione's last and Titian's early works so controversial, and the borderline so blurred. And yet, the problem must be solved, however knotty it may be. That it is troublesome was recognized on the occasion of the Giorgione exhibition in Venice in 1955, when such masterpieces as the *Concert* by the young Titian (Plate 4) had to be exhibited under the Giorgione label.

In comparing the characteristics of Giorgione's unquestioned paintings such as the *Madonna of Castelfranco*, the *Tempest*, and the *Three Philosophers* (to name only some of the major works), with pictures by the young Titian which are controversial, namely, the *Sleeping Venus* (Figure 1) in Dresden, the *Concert* (Louvre), and the other version in the Pitti Palace, the spirit of the latter group is Giorgionesque, but it is less enchanted, absorbed or given to reverie. Whereas Giorgione's figures parallel the picture surface, Titian's are placed in the landscape, fused with the natural cosmos in accordance with Aristotelian philosophy current at the school of Padua. In Titian's paintings, figures enhance the landscape; they hardly stay in the confines of the canvas, so much so that paintings such as the *Fête Champêtre* (Plate 1) and the *Deposition* (Plate 13) (both in the Louvre) and others were later enlarged in order to give the figures more space; conversely, Titian intended them to dominate the space; by their physical presence, breaking out of their erstwhile containment.

Titian was barely twenty years old according to Dolce when he assisted Giorgione in painting the frescoes of the Fondaco dei Tedeschi, the master doing the more important façade facing the Grand Canal, his pupil the side walls of the palace facing the magazines. These murals were Titian's first public commission, and unfortunately, all that remains are some engravings made after the originals by Zanetti in 1760 and a fresco fragment detached from the wall in very poor condition, now in the Ducal Palace. Yet even these meager remnants convey an idea of the artist's early creative power when in 1508 he was turning twenty years. Contemporary biographers note that Titian's success in this assignment aroused the jealousy of his friend and master Giorgione, and we may assume that after the episode of the Fondaco murals relations between the two artists deteriorated, perhaps to the point of a complete break. Now a celebrated painter in Venice, Titian advanced rapidly, and two years later was commissioned to paint the murals of the Scuola del Santo in Padua, in the very year of Giorgione's premature death (1510).

What work by Titian preceded the Fondaco murals? Surely he must have proven his talents prior to this time, for Dolce says that by " drawing and painting with Giorgione he soon became so proficient in art " as to be considered worthy of assisting his master in the fresco paintings. Obviously we are forced to conjecture and draw conclusions from some graphic documents as, for instance, the volume of engravings published by Le Febre in 1682. These are chiefly landscape and figure compositions, allegedly by Titian, clearly inspired by Giorgione, and showing some influence from Domenico Campagnola. The young Titian also appears to have been inspired especially by the mysterious, fantastic landscapes of Durer who visited Venice in 1506. Indeed, interest in landscape painting had grown steadily during the first decade of the 16th century and, with the memory of the scenic beauty of his native Cadore fresh in his youthful mind, Titian consequently developed in his early years a strong predilection for landscape painting which reasserted itself, though less vigorously, in the years of his maturity and old age. His

12

Fig. 8. *Portrait of a Man Wearing a Plumed Hat.* Egremont, Petworth House.

landscapes won him early fame and the unanimous praise of his biographers, the first being his contemporary Paolo Pino (1548).

On the basis of the engravings made by Le Febre and on Titian's subsequent development, we may mention as Titian's early works two paintings in the Padua museum, the *Birth of Adonis*, and the *Forest of Polydorus*, both executed with boldness, intensely colorful, and forceful in expression. To these we may add the *Sleeping Endymion* (Barnes Foundation in Merion, Pennsylvania), showing the same exquisitely lyrical feeling for landscape. These were soon followed by the *Orpheus and Eurydice* (Carrara Gallery, Bergamo), a painting once attributed to Giorgione but now recognized almost unanimously as a work of the young Titian. These works of a slightly archaic quality are inconceivable without Giorgione's precedent, but their poetic conception is more dramatic, and the color has a richer impasto. Limitations of space do not permit me to discuss other works which the artist must have painted between the time of his apprenticeship with Giorgione and the execution of the Fondaco murals. In these murals Titian did not include landscape motifs; the human figure prevailed in a new forcefulness, full of vitality and energy. A comparison of Titian's and Giorgione's figures in these frescoes reveals the new trend in Venetian painting already in the early years of the 16th century.

*   *   *

Titian's new direction is shown also by the frescoes in the Scuola del Santo, Padua, done two years later (1511) and luckily still preserved intact. These leave no doubt as to the true ambition of the young artist who by then had extricated himself completely from the spell of the great fathers of Venetian painting, Giovanni Bellini and Giorgione. It is impossible to overemphasize the importance of the Padua frescoes in the history of Venetian art, comparable as they are to the Florentine art of Masaccio in the Brancacci Chapel almost a century earlier. A new pictorial world was introduced in these frescoes executed within a few months. The miracles of Saint Anthony in Padua were painted by Titian in vivid movement, realistic, yet powerful and concise, in a manner then unprecedented in the art of painting. In the first episode, *Saint Anthony Granting Speech to an Infant* (Plates 2, 3), enabling him to bear witness to his mother's innocence, we admire not only the new rhythm of the free composition but also the characterization of individual figures, their dignified appearance, and the moving expression of their feelings reflected in gestures and faces. In the *Miracle of the Woman Killed by her Jealous Husband*, the painter's interest is not focused on the resuscitated woman (who is, in fact, relegated to the background as a secondary figure) but on the intensely dramatic scene of the man stabbing his wife. Titian had made detailed preparatory drawings for the fresco, one of which is preserved in the Ecole des Beaux-Arts in Paris (Figure 29). In the third fresco, the *Miracle of the Reattached Foot*, there is great dignity and nobility in the figures, and a greater narrative conciseness. In each of these scenes, landscape reappears in all its suggestive power and fascinating lyricism.

These frescoes of the Scuola del Santo in Padua vividly demonstrate Titian's new approach to the function of color. It is no longer additional to drawing; it is used for

14

Fig. 9. *Assumption of the Virgin*. Venice, Sta. Maria dei Frari.

its own sake, as the means of creating form, applied in patches with rapid, decisive strokes to be viewed from afar rather than from nearby. Needless to say this marks the beginning of modern painting in the larger meaning of the term.

Between the time when the murals of the Fondaco and those in Padua were painted, Titian must have made a number of pictures in a style that bridges the period of time, separating these two series. However, in the absence of documentary proof we must proceed cautiously, relying entirely on the evidence of the works themselves, which, as mentioned above, are still being attributed by some scholars to Giorgione's late period.

To begin with there is still the unsolved problem of the *Sleeping Venus* in Dresden (Figure 1). If this is the painting seen by Michiel in the house of Marcello in 1523, described by him as being " by the hand of Zorzo, except that the landscape and Cupid (now overpainted) was finished by Titian," we can imagine that Titian did not confine himself to finishing the picture but repainted it completely. Perhaps more plausible is Fogolari's hypothesis that Michiel saw a different picture, one in which Venus was seen from the back. Leaving aside this rather doubtful documentary evidence, the painting seems to have all the characteristics of a work by Titian. The dominance of the figure in the landscape, the bold handling of the deeply creased drapery which contrasts with Giorgione's softer treatment, the sky with its large white clouds, the stronger, richer handling — are all indications that the painting should be attributed to Titian. The argument that the face of Venus is thinner and more languid than that of women painted by Titian may be countered by noting that in his early works Titian was still under the influence of Giorgione. Similarly imbued with the lyrical spirit of Giorgione is the *Fête Champêtre* in the Louvre (Plate 1), in which Titian's artistic individuality is disclosed in the relationship between figures and landscape, the former overlapping the latter, the richer impasto of color, and the modelling of the figures, some of which reappear shortly afterwards in the Padua frescoes. There is a stylistic affinity connecting this extremely beautiful work and the soft, fluid handling of the *Noli me tangere* in the National Gallery, London (Figure 5). The dramatically moving figure of the *Adulteress* in Glasgow, which resembles the figures in the Padua frescoes, is in marked contrast to Giorgione's contemplative and serene figures. Similar pictorial handling is discernible in the *Madonna with Saints Roch and Anthony* in the Prado (Figure 2) which, though still under Bellini's influence and reminiscent of Giorgione's Castelfranco altarpiece, presents an entirely new feeling for color in closer harmonies and in a superior majesty of form.

Among the works once attributed to Giorgione's mature style, but now recognized almost unanimously as by the young Titian, are the *Christ and the Rascal* in the Scuola di San Rocco, the so-called *Gypsy Woman* in Vienna which, though larger and more sensual, resembles the *Madonna* in the Prado, and, finally, the wonderful *Concert* in the Pitti Palace (Plate 4). The dramatic impact of the latter is evident in the vitality of their physical presence, communicated to the viewer in a flash of harmonious rhythms. Here we see Titian's marvelous grasp of reality, his skill in catching and rendering a fleeting moment, a glance, a gesture in its most essential aspect, all rendered with the spontaneity and vitality that is characteristic of his entire art. The nervous play of the strong hands touching the keys of the harpsichord, the attentive attitude of the viola

16

Fig. 10. Polyptych, *Resurrection of Christ*. Brescia, SS. Nazzaro e Celso.

player, the atmosphere of tension and restrained vitality — all this is rendered by Titian with consummate intuition.

This review of Titian's early work may detract from Giorgione's œuvre but it does not in any way diminish his fame; it does, however, demonstrate his pupil's bolder and more sanguine art. This is borne out by the artist's other works of the period: for instance, his numerous portraits and the *Altarpiece with Five Saints*, in Santa Maria della Salute, probably intended as an ex-voto after the plague of 1510 which took Giorgione's life.

The portraits painted by the young Titian are deserving of special attention. The frescoes in the Scuola del Santo have already revealed the painter's ability to grasp the

17

character of his models. These are portraits of living persons, individuals in all their vitality. These lively portraits are not generalized or vague types. One easily imagines that he had painted portraits from the beginning. In fact, a number of portraits may be placed during his Padua period and shortly thereafter. The two musicians of the *Concert* (Pitti Palace) are portraits just as is the Saint Ulfo in the *Sacred Conversation* (Prado); according to an acceptable tradition with which I would agree, it is considered the artist's self-portrait. Perhaps the same person appears in the painting in the National Gallery in London which is supposed to represent *Ariosto* (Figure 4). In this work, which is still Giorgionesque in conception and spirit, an identification with the poet or the nobleman of the Casa Barbarigo appears doubtful. Other paintings from the period of the Padua frescoes are the *Portrait of a Youth*, who rests his glove-clad hand on a parapet, (Figure 6), in the collection of the Earl of Halifax, London, the recently discovered *Youth with a Plumed Hat* in Petworth House, Egremont (Figure 8), and the *Man in a Red Cap* in the Frick Collection (Figure 7), inexplicably contested by some scholars, and yet in my opinion one of the most perfect manifestations of the young Titian's skill as a portraitist. I have little doubt that the two latter paintings and still others, including the harpsichord player in the *Concert* (Pitti) represent the same person. Regarding the possibility that it may be a portrait of Giorgione, especially when compared with his self-portrait in Braunschweig, the hypothesis was advanced by me years ago. These two paintings share a profound psychological individuality which goes beyond formal presentation and exceptionally fine painterly qualities. The handling is fluid, softly fused in the passages of color and light, strokes seemingly applied with delicate feather rather than with a brush.

The *Portrait of a Musician* in the Spada Gallery, Rome (Plate 7) is somewhat uneven in quality, perhaps because it seems to have been left at the sketch stage. This mysterious portrait of great poetic intensity was once attributed to Giorgione but reclaimed by me for Titian. The handsome face reminds us once again of Titian's own features. The *Man with a Glove* in the Louvre (Plate 8) and the *Portrait of Vincenzo Mosti* in the Pitti Palace (Plate 9) are works of profound concentration which belong to a later period.

* * *

Titian's early portraits are almost all of men. An exception is the *Schiavona* (Slavic Woman) in the National Gallery, London, a finely individual portrait painted from life. This woman may have been the model for the Padua fresco, *Saint Anthony Grants Speech to an Infant* (Plate 3) where she is shown in profile and slightly idealized. On the other hand, the famous images of *Violante* (Vienna), the *Salome* (Doria Pamphili Gallery, Rome) and the *Flora* (Uffizi), to name only the principal ones, appear to be idealizations rather than actual portraits.

For paintings of madonnas, biblical subjects, and allegories, Titian conceived a type of feminine beauty whose guiding influence is felt throughout and beyond the 16th century. Instead of the young, slender, delicate and pensive woman of remote Gothic ancestry found in Giorgione's pictures, Titian's are more earthly, robust and sensual. There is an affinity between this innovation in feminine beauty and Michelangelo's new type of heroic women, even though they may differ in effect.

18

Fig. 11. *Madonna of the Pesaro Family*. Venice, Sta. Maria dei Frari.

These new formal conceptions by Titian are embodied in the famous masterpiece *Sacred and Profane Love* in the Borghese Gallery (Plates 5 and 6) painted ca. 1515, a few years after the Padua frescoes. The meaning of this picture is a riddle which scholars have yet to resolve. Perhaps it has something to do with the opposition of contrasting principles — Good and Evil or Virtue and Vice — as presented during the Middle Ages and the Renaissance. Some years before Titian's painting, Aldo Manuzio had published Fra Francesco Colonna's novel, *Hypnerotomachia Poliphilii*; its illustrations were popular among the elite of Venetian artists as a storehouse of pictorial themes. Certain parallels with the book suggest a partial influence on Titian who may have intended to illustrate the meeting of Venus and Polia, the novel's heroine. When the picture entered the collection of Scipione Borghese in the early 17th century, it was called " Beauty adorned and unadorned, " a title which seems to me to be most appropriate for this painting justly considered one of the greatest works in the history of art. As in Titian's *Concert*, the women in this painting seem to be engaged in a silent dialogue as they sit on the edge of an antique fountain in the water of which a little boy is playing. What captures our imagination is not the unexpressed words, or the narrative content, but rather the spell of the poetic enchantment of Beauty in the human form and in nature, the tangible atmosphere of a revelation that is perfect in every detail and brings us to the pinnacle of artistic creation. Even Phidias's sculpture is excelled by the gentle, mysterious, harmony of the two figures, absorbed as they are in the late afternoon atmosphere of a landscape that is rich in mysterious accents, and Giorgionesque in the detail of the castle tower touched gently by the last rays from the setting sun. Granting that the theme of the painting derives from literature, nevertheless its poetry transcends the purest visual delight.

In these years, or shortly before, Titian painted the *Sacred Conversation* in the Balbi Gallery, Genoa (Figure 3), a work of equal beauty and poetic feeling. The monumental figure of the Madonna fills almost the entire space, except for the area to the right where two male figures are set before a landscape which is Giorgionesque in inspiration. The sweet, blond Saint Catherine, so reminiscent of Palma Vecchio, and the serenity of the Child are innovations in religious painting where sacred and secular elements are so interrelated as to form a new interpretation of the subject. The drapery is arranged in harmonious rhythms, rich in color and in plasticity. While it enhances the volumes of the figures, it also has its own significance as the means of heightening its artistic essence. Alternately light and heavy folds fall in a lively fluctuating cascade, creating shadow-filled areas and mysterious, chromatic vibrations.

Leonardo had already made detailed studies of drapery effects and his clothed figures reveal a constant preoccupation with the faithful rendering of fabrics. That Giorgione had been equally conscious of this problem is seen in his *Holy Family* (formerly in the Benson collection; now in the National Gallery, Washington), where the bold play of the folds in the Virgin's cloak spread out like a Gothic flower design. Titian soon abandoned the Gothic elements of Giorgione who had been inspired by Northern engravings. True his early paintings occasionally show traces of Giorgione's drapery effects, but a broader, classic conception is evident in the Padua frescoes. Although Gothic archaisms are still

20

Fig. 12. *Bacchus and Ariadne.* London, National Gallery.

noticeable in the composition of the *Triumph of Faith* (1508), they soon disappeared in the further development of his graphic art.

In 1513, soon after Titian had completed the Padua murals, he received an invitation from Pietro Bembo to come to Rome to the court of Pope Leo X — a great distinction which the young artist, nevertheless, declined. He preferred to remain in Venice where he proposed to the Council of Ten to paint a battle scene for the Hall of the Great Council in exchange for being given the first broker's patent that would be vacant in the Fondaco dei Tedeschi. The patent was granted at once, then revoked in 1514, and finally accorded once again in 1517 when Giovanni Bellini who held title to the patent died in 1516. Regarding the *Balbi Madonna*, we may add that its religious atmosphere of a Sacred Conversation corresponds to the Bellini tradition of a poetic, homelike intimacy. There can be no doubt as to the sincerity of Titian's religious feelings, for it is manifest in all his religious paintings and was intensified as he advanced in years.

21

Fig. 13. *Portrait of Francesco Acquaviva, Duke of Atri.* (?) Kassel, Gallery.

Fig. 14. *Portrait of Don Diego Mendoza.* Florence, Pitti Palace.

Truly indicative of Titian's religiousness is the *Baptism of Christ* (Capitoline Museum, Rome), a work that has been denied him by some scholars, but which is, in my opinion, undoubtedly by his hand. The addition of the donor in the lower part of the painting strikes a rather archaic note, but its place in the composition is evidently due to the donor's request. Christ stands knee-deep in the stream which flows through a poignant landscape. The contrapposto of John the Baptist is a pre-Mannerist conception. Christ is absorbed in prayer, deeply conscious of the sacrament, and an expression of restrained sadness covers His face. This painting, meticulous in design, its smallest details finely rendered, belongs to the painter's early period and may be dated ca. 1512-1515. The handling of the landscape corresponds to that in *Sacred and Profane Love* (Plates 5 and 6).

We may place in this period another outstanding example of Titian's religious painting, the *Tribute Money* (Dresden), as well as the *Madonna with the Cherries* (Vienna).

The painting which added enormously to Titian's fame was the *Assumption of the Virgin* for the Church of the Frari (Figure 9). The praise by his contemporaries for this work still astounds us; its impact on Venetian art must have been staggering. Commissioned by the prior of the Monastery of the Frari in 1516, this magnificent picture was solemnly installed on the high altar on March 20, 1518. All Venetians came to admire it.

22

The words of Dolce indicate the importance attributed from the outset to this masterpiece by Titian then barely thirty years old: "It is a miracle that Titian, who is unfamiliar with the antiquities of Rome by which all eminent painters have been inspired, and who was guided by the little inspiration he discovered in Giorgione's works, has seen and brought the art of painting to such perfection. "

The tremendous impact of this stupendous painting on artists and public alike can only be explained by comparing it with the paintings of Titian's predecessors, Giovanni Bellini and his followers Cima da Conigliano, the brothers Basaiti, and Vincenzo Catena, to name only the greatest. Titian's altarpiece, when compared with the works of these traditionalists, stands out as an incredible, unprecedented achievement. A new vigor is released in the sensuous, sparkling colors, the plastic corporeality of the figures, and the highly dramatic dynamism bursting with life. This was a new way of painting, one of vibration, movement, and vigorous energy, previously unknown in Venetian painting or elsewhere in Europe.

II.

With all the excitement which the *Assumption* had aroused among connoisseurs and enlightened public, Titian's contemporaries were equally fascinated by three Bacchanalian Scenes painted for the Alabaster Chamber of Alfonso d'Este. Vasari calls them " works of rare quality, executed with incredible diligence. " Indeed, these three works of a flawless design, bright and translucent colors, and inspired by classical sources are among Titian's most delightful creations. They are entirely worthy of the distinguished place which they were intended to decorate. The *Worship of Venus,* now in the Prado (Plate 10), consists of a host of carousing putti. It was the first of three Bacchanalian scenes and was completed between April, 1518 and October, 1519. Titian's second picture was the *Bacchanal* (Plates 11, 12) in which he extols the river of drunkeness which flows through the happy island of Andros like Lethe, the river of oblivion. The *Bacchus and Ariadne* in the National Gallery, London (Figure 12), begun in 1522 and finished in 1523, was the third canvas in the series. Here classicism found its noblest interpreter. Bacchus seems like a Greek statue suddenly freed from its marble casing and bursting with the elixir of life through Titian's vigorous art. The profound poetic spirit evoked in these three paintings, based on the texts of Philostratus and Catullus, set an admirable pattern for 17th century painting, ranging from Domenichino to Poussin and Rubens. Alfonso d'Este, Duke of Ferrara, apparently decided to give the commission of the Bacchanalian Scenes to Titian when he had difficulty in obtaining for his chamber some work by the divine Raphael, whom he had overwhelmed with requests through his ambassador, Constabili. To satisfy the Duke, to whom he had long promised a *Triumph of Bacchus*, Raphael sent him the cartoon of the *Battle of Ostia* in November, 1517, the cartoon of *Saint Michael*, in November, 1518 and, in 1519, the *Portrait of Joan of Aragon*, now in Paris. These pictures by Raphael in Ferrara provided an opportunity for Titian, who frequently visited there in those years, to acquire a firsthand knowledge of Raphael's art and to experience its charm. It has been noted in fact that in Titian's altarpiece in Ancona, dated 1520, there are traces of Raphaelesque inspiration, especially since the *Madonna and the Child Enthroned on a Cloud* has a slight hint of Raphael's *Madonna of Foligno*. However, the rest of the altarpiece — the bright sky with its dazzling white clouds, the statuesque figures of Saints Francis and Alvise, the solemn portrait of the donor, and richly moist colors in the landscape are Titian's own.

Reminiscences of a Raphaelesque composition linger in Titian's *Deposition* in the Louvre, painted probably for Isabella d'Este or the Marquis of Mantua ca. 1525 (Plate 13). Nevertheless its pictorial conception is fundamentally different, for its towering figures almost fill the entire canvas. Interestingly enough, the original spacial arrangement was altered when, at some later time, strips of canvas were added along the upper and lower edges.

Titian's new art and its brilliant inventiveness brought him an increasing number of commissions forcing him early in his career to cope with limitations of time, controversies with aristocratic patrons of art, and keeping up with continuous requests for paintings. Some of these delicate problems were resolved by his own diplomatic talents, while later in his life he availed himself, in addition to his own innate diplomatic skill, of Pietro Aretino whose facility with words frequently proved of great help in Titian's dealings with important patrons. To Alfonso d'Este who menacingly insisted on having the Bacchanalian scenes, Titian offered a part of a polyptych which had been commissioned in 1520 by the papal envoy in Venice, Altobello Averoldi. This was the *Saint Sebastian*. But the Duke did not dare to accept for fear of incurring the enmity of the papal envoy. Titian completed the polyptych two years later in 1522, adding his signature and the date, and sent it to the Church of San Nazzaro and San Celso in Brescia. The altarpiece (Figure 10) shows the Resurrection of Christ in the center, Saint Sebastian and the titular saints with the donor Averoldi in the lower side panels, and the Annunciation in the upper panels. Here Titian's art unfolds in all its power. Painted in strong chiaroscuro, the figures have the plasticity of Michelangelo's work and a strong formal conception. The central scene of the Resurrection is especially impressive for its dramatic contrasts of light and dark. The figure of Christ rises majestically against the sky, illuminated by a supernatural light and the rose-colored glow of dawn spreading over the horizon, while the warrior in the foreground is enveloped by shadow. This polyptych paved the way for the Brescia school of painting during the 16th century, influencing Savoldo above all, but also Moretto and Romanino and their followers.

Titian presented a new type of altarpiece in his *Madonna of the Pesaro Family* for the Church of the Frari. The *Assumption* had hardly been unveiled when Jacopo Pesaro, Bishop of Paphos, in charge of the papal galleries, commissioned him to do an altarpiece for the Altar of the Conception in the Church of the Frari. The contract was signed on April 24, 1519, but the altarpiece was not unveiled until December 8, 1526. This majestic painting, which constitutes a new design in altarpieces and later profoundly influenced van Dyck, reveals Titian's enormously inventive talents. The figures kneeling in prayer at the bottom, the Madonna on a raised throne, and the restless putto are all part of a rhythmic movement in a grandiose space, directed toward the heavens where two giant columns partly conceal a luminous sky.

Fig. 15. *Venus of Pardo.* Paris, Louvre.

After the sack of Rome in 1527, Pietro Aretino, the "world's secretary," was a newcomer seeking refuge in Venice. He is said to have remarked with unheard-of arrogance that the treads of his stairs were as much worn out by the footsteps of famous visitors as was the pavement of the Capitoline in Rome by the wheels of triumphal carriages. This controversial libelist soon became Titian's friend, immediately took charge of the artist's relations with his influential patrons, and sought to spread the painter's fame far and wide, wherever his redoubtable pen reached. No doubt it was Aretino's suggestion that prompted Titian in 1527 to send to Federigo Gonzaga, with whom he had been in contact since 1523, portraits of Aretino and Girolamo Adorno, the ambassador of Charles V. The Marquis of Mantua responded with thanks, money, and the promise of further demonstrations of esteem and sympathy.

While these two portraits are no longer identifiable, others from the same period reveal Titian's continued development in portraiture. Once he had abandoned the Giorgionesque concept of mystic reverie, he continued to stress the psychological aspects of his sitters, endowing them with a new expression of dignified composure which emphasized their noble and lofty station. In Titian's portraits the human figure is also endowed with greater plasticity. There are two splendid portraits of Federigo Gonzaga which are forceful, monumental, and broadly modelled; the one in the Prado representing the Marquis with his dog, and another in the Omaha Museum which includes a hunter's falcon. These two portraits, originally in the collection of the Marquis of Mantua, were painted after 1523, the year of Titian's first contact with the court of Mantua. The Gonzaga collection included the *Portrait of a Man* (Louvre), which was once believed to represent Aretino. It shares with a portrait in the Munich Museum a breadth of composition that suggests a dating ca. 1523.

The year 1527 saw the arrival in Venice of Jacopo Sansovino, who soon became a

25

friend of Titian. Michelangelo's visit to Venice in 1529 contributed further to the spread of cultural influences from Rome which had been felt in Venice for years. It has been stated — incorrectly in my opinion — that Michelangelo's presence influenced Titian's conception of the altarpiece of *Saint Peter Martyr*, a painting of great fame unfortunately destroyed in 1867. In 1528 Titian won a contest in competition with Palma Vecchio and Pordenone, sponsored by the Brotherhood, to paint an altarpiece for the Church of San Giovanni e Paolo. The enthusiastic descriptions by contemporary and later biographers and the numerous engravings of this altarpiece which was installed on April 27, 1530, serve to emphasize its importance. From one painting to the next Titian achieved a more dramatic effect; first by enlarging the human figure to the point of nearly eliminating surrounding space and landscape, and later by a gradually accentuated plasticism. But in this altarpiece he has found a violently dynamic solution in which the equalizing function of the landscape has been restored. A solution which, though based on certain Roman presuppositions, remains removed from the art of Michelangelo and the mannerism of his followers.

* * *

Political events in Italy had taken a turn which was to have a fundamental influence on Titian's art and life. The power of Charles V continued to grow after his victory over Francis I at Pavia and his meeting with Pope Clement VII in Bologna at the end of 1529, by whom he was crowned on February 30, 1530. Through Aretino's skillful machinations, the benevolent efforts of the Marquis of Mantua, who was then Titian's most important patron, and the fame which his works had gained him, Titian was in Bologna probably early in 1530 to paint a portrait of Charles V which is now lost. This marked the beginning of Titian's subsequent and fortunate relations with Charles V which were to have an enormous influence on his career.

In February, 1530, Giacomo Malatesta wrote to Federigo Gonzaga that Titian had shown him the paintings for the Marquis on which he was working: one, *Our Lady with Saint Catherine;* and the other, *Female Nudes*. Nothing is known today about the second, but the former is now generally identified with the *Madonna with the Rabbit* in the Louvre (Plate 15). It has something of Giorgione's poetic charm, soft handling, rich color, and light rhythm. According to tradition, the lovely face of the Madonna is that of the artist's young wife Cecilia who died in 1530. From this union, legitimized by marriage in 1525, Titian had three children: a daughter, Lavinia; Orazio, who became a painter; and Pomponio, who embarked on an unsuccessful ecclesiastic career and frequently grieved his father by his turbulent activities.

In 1530-1531 Titian apparently continued to work for the Marquis of Mantua, then his most important patron. In addition to a *Saint Sebastian,* now lost but allegedly similar to that in the polyptych commissioned by Altobello Averoldi, Titian sent the Marquis a painting of *Saint Jerome* in March, 1531, generally believed to be the painting now in the Louvre. Indeed, the latter was once in the collection in Mantua and stylistically it should be placed ca. 1531. St. Jerome is shown praying in the silence of a forest, whose dark masses of tall trees set off against a reddish sky recall those in the *Saint Peter Martyr*.

26

Fig. 16. *Portrait of Clarice Strozzi.* Berlin, Staatliche Museen.

In *Saint Jerome* the landscape takes on a larger role, rendered with great economy of means and yet deeply moving in content; in this respect there is a faint echo of Lorenzo Lotto.

Through Benedetto Agnello's correspondence with Federigo Gonzaga we know that in 1531 Titian was working on a painting of the *Magdalene* which the Marquis intended to present to Vittoria Colonna. Some scholars have identified this picture with the version now at the Pitti Gallery, while others believe it is the work described by Vasari as a " bust of Saint Mary Magdalene with short hair, rarely so depicted " which he saw in the collection of the Duke of Urbino. We know from Titian himself that the version of this subject which he painted for the Marquis of Mantua showed the saint with her " hands at her breast. "

The *Supper at Emmaus* (Louvre) was once believed to have been painted for Gonzaga, but study of the painting has uncovered the coat of arms of the Maffei family by whom it must therefore have been commissioned. The same subject is in the collection at Brocklesby Park.

Titian's work for Gonzaga won him, in 1531, the parish of Medole for his son Pomponio for whose church the artist later painted a *Christ Appearing to his Mother* (1554) which unfortunately since then has deteriorated.

In the autumn of 1531 Titian left the studio he had occupied since 1513 at San Samuele, and, having hired Antonio Buxei and Ludovico di Giovanni as his assistants, moved to San Canciano at Birri Grande where he rented first a part, then later in 1536, the entire Casa Grande. Situated as it was out on the lagoon, the house had a marvelous vista extending to the distant mountains. Every visitor praised the house and especially the garden. Priscianese described it in 1540 as " located on the sea at the far end of Venice, where one sees the charming island of Murano and other most beautiful places."

In 1531 Titian furnished a votive painting of the newly elected Doge Andrea Gritti for the Sala del Collegio in the Ducal Palace. Sanudo saw it on display when he visited the place on October 6 of that year. Highly praised by contemporary biographers, this picture was destroyed in the fire of 1577 and is known to us only from an engraving. It shows Saint Mark presenting the doge to the Virgin, as Saints Bernardino, Alvise, and Marina debate before the Virgin their respective merits in the election of the new doge, following a tradition that was current in Titian's time.

In November, 1532, Charles V came to Italy to attend to major political problems, passing through Ferrara and Mantua on his way to Bologna. A visit to Federigo Gonzaga in Mantua gave the Emperor an opportunity to admire the art treasures assembled at that magnificent court. Profoundly impressed by Titian's portrait of the Marquis, he expressed a desire to sit again for the great Venetian painter. Hastily summoned by Gonzaga, Titian joined the Emperor in Bologna, and there, during the months of December, 1532 to February, 1533, he painted him for the second time. In this portrait, generally believed to be the one in the Prado, Charles V is shown in full figure, dressed in a gorgeous costume of state and holding a big dog by the collar with his left hand. Tradition has it that the effect of the portrait on the august patron was such that he refused ever to be painted again by anyone but Titian. From Barcelona on May 10, 1533, the Emperor conferred on

Fig. 17. *Charles V on Horseback*. Madrid, Prado.

him the titles of Count Palatine and Knight of the Golden Spur as a token of his esteem, and in appreciation of his genius named him the Apelles of his time.

Vasari relates that while in Bologna Titian also painted the portrait of Cardinal Ippolito de Medici, a powerful and highly influential figure at the imperial court, who became henceforth an eager patron and protector of the artist. The Cardinal, a person of much stronger military than ecclesiastical inclinations, wished to be portrayed in Hungarian dress in recognition of his recent return from the war in Hungary. The portrait, now in the Pitti Palace, is, indeed, one of the most unusual examples of Titian's ability to capture the character of his sitter.

In 1534 Isabella d'Este, then a lady of mature age, asked Titian to paint her as a young lady, and to this end sent him a portrait done by Francesco Francia many years earlier. The painting of the Duchess which Titian delivered in 1536 has been identified unanimously with that in the Kunsthistorisches Museum, Vienna, in which Isabella is shown sumptuously dressed in all the charm and splendor of her youth.

However, Titian's masterpiece in portraiture of this decade is the so-called *Bella* in the Pitti Palace (Plate 17). We know from the Duke's correspondence with his representative, Giacomo Leonardi, that it was painted for the Duke of Urbino in 1536. The girl's lavish costume does not detract in any way from the supreme beauty and natural simplicity of this young woman, whose portrait was to become the ideal for artists of the High Renaissance. The same young woman, who remains anonymous, is represented in the *Young Woman in a Fur* (Kunsthistorisches Museum, Vienna) and in the *Young Woman with a Feather Hat* (Hermitage, Leningrad). Their stylistic affinity with the *Bella* suggests that they were painted in the same period.

It is interesting that Charles V's patronage of Titian during this time did not prevent the diplomatically shrewd artist from portraying the Emperor's archenemy, Francis I of France. The King's portrait, now in the Louvre, is believed to be the one completed in 1538, after a medallion made by Benvenuto Cellini. Among the portraits painted by Titian during the 1530's, we should mention also that of *Antonio Porcia* (Brera, Milan) and those of certain members of Charles V's court, namely, the artillery commander *Gabriele Tadino* (Bendit Collection, New York), and the *Marquis del Vasto Alfonso d'Avalos* (de Ganay collection, Paris). The latter was finished probably during Titian's second stay in Bologna in 1532-1533. The Marquis del Vasto, whom Titian painted again later with his son in the famous *Allocution of Alfonso d'Avalos* (Plate 21), was a passionate art collector and Titian's great admirer. An unverified tradition holds that Titian painted for him the *Allegory* in the Louvre, and his biographers have claimed to recognize in the painting the Marquis himself departing for war against the Turks (1532) and bidding farewell to his wife Mary of Aragon in the presence of Cupid, Victory, and Hymen.

Between 1534 and 1538 Titian executed the largest canvas he had ever undertaken, the *Presentation in the Temple*, now in the Academy, for the Brotherhood of Santa Maria della Carità in Venice (Plate 16). Compositionally, the painting is reminiscent of the work of the Bellinis and of Carpaccio; indeed, something similar may be seen in Jacopo Bellini's sketchbook nearly a century earlier. In Titian's painting, however, almost the entire canvas is filled with monumental architecture, except for a glimpse of the blue

Fig. 18. *Votive Portrait of the Vendramin Family.* London, National Gallery.

sky and the mountains of Marmarole which are those of his birthplace. Titian has portrayed the event with extraordinary freshness and has introduced elements from the local Venetian scene. In place of the Pharisees who witnessed the Virgin's presentation, Titian has represented the impressive dignitaries of Venice, capturing all with utmost naturalness. Among many naturalistic motifs, perhaps the most outstanding is the old woman with a basket of eggs seated at the side of the staircase.

When Francesco Maria della Rovere, Duke of Urbino, became commander in chief of the Venetian forces in 1532, he met Titian and commissioned him to do three paintings, the subjects being an image of *Christ*, a *Nativity*, and a *Portrait of Hannibal*. However, not until November, 1534, after many pleas for the pictures, did the Duke finally succeed in receiving the *Nativity*, and he wrote from Pesaro that he was extremely pleased with it. There is some disagreement as to the identification of this painting with the *Nativity* in the Pitti Palace, but, the splendid quality of the work, despite its poor condition, should dispel all doubts regarding authorship. A few months later, in 1535, the *Portrait of Hannibal* and the *Christ* were completed. The portrait has been lost, and the painting of *Christ* in the Pitti is another version of a more famous one in Dresden, showing Him in profile against the background of an evening landscape.

In addition to the *Bella* and the *Magdalene* (Pitti), Titian painted portraits of the Duke and Duchess of Urbino in 1536 and 1538. We know from the Duchess' letter that

31

the Duke's portrait was received in Pesaro in April, 1538. In the *Francesco Maria della Rovere*, now in the Uffizi, Titian presents a vivid portrait of the condottiere in shining armor, commanding in a sweeping gesture. In contrast to the portrait of Federigo Gonzaga in the Prado, where Titian is interested in the silhouette, in this portrait he takes up the problem of the space occupied by the figure. The conception is one of grandeur, and the helmet and arms behind the Duke make the ambient all the more tangible. This was a device which he repeated in some of his later portraits, notably that of Jacopo Strada (Plate 31). A vigorous and concise pen drawing in the Uffizi shows Titian's original idea of painting the Duke of Urbino in full length. By April, 1538, the *Portrait of Eleonora Gonzaga*, Duchess of Urbino, had also reached Pesaro; in 1631 it came to the Uffizi from the Della Rovere estate. The Duchess is shown in three-quarter length, an austere and dignified, but somewhat solemn woman. Evidently she did not inspire the artist's imagination, for the portrait lacks the vigor of its companion piece.

Francesco Maria della Rovere died in 1537 and was succeeded by Guidobaldo with whom Titian had already been in contact when he was Duke of Camerino. For Guidobaldo, Titian executed one of his most famous paintings, the so-called *Venus of Urbino*, now in the Uffizi (Plate 18), peremptorily ordered by the Duke to be collected by a special envoy in March, 1538. Comparable in its miraculous pictorial perfection to the marvellous *Bacchanal*, this glowing nude is, however, more vibrant, sensuous, and plastic than the earlier painting. Although referred to as *Venus*, this picture may not originally have been conceived as such by the artist. Responding to a deep attraction, Titian may have yielded here to an impulse inspired by a subject of universal appeal — a "nude woman," as the painting is called in Guidobaldo's records. Because her face is identical to that of the *Bella*, the picture has been presumed to represent the Duke's paramour, at least so it is said by Vasari. By contrast to the *Sleeping Venus* (Figure 1) in Dresden, painted by Titian some thirty years earlier in a Giorgionesque style and set in a lyrical landscape, the *Venus of Urbino* is placed in an interior space in the depth of which appear two servants looking into a chest.

Titian's proverbial slowness in carrying out his commissions finally resulted in a sharp conflict with Venetian authorities. These worthies had entrusted the painting of the Library in the Ducal Palace to Pordenone in November, 1538, and considering his efficiency were inclined to award him also the commission adjacent to the space in the Hall of the Great Council which Titian was supposed to have filled with his *Battle*, promised since 1513. As retribution for his failure to deliver (in fact some twenty-four years had elapsed since he first offered to paint the *Battle*), Titian was deprived of the broker's patent at the Fondaco dei Tedeschi. Still, he was not shaken out of his indolence until June 23, 1537 when the Council of Ten requested him to refund the money he had collected for the broker's patent during all these years. A year later, in August, 1538, he had finished the work which unfortunately perished in the fire of 1577, leaving us only Fontana's engraving of it made in 1569 and another anonymous one in the Albertina, Vienna.

Vasari called this battle scene the *Rout of Chiaradadda;* Sansovino referred to it in 1581 as the *Battle of Spoleto*, and Ridolfi in 1648 as the *Battle of Cadore*. Ridolfi says,

32

Fig. 19. *Pietro Aretino*. Florence, Pitti Palace.

" He depicted his own country with mountains topped by a castle which, set afire by lightning, shoots forth dark, globe-shaped clouds in the midst of a horrible storm, while the fields are crowded with knights and foot-soldiers engaged in a ferocious battle, some with their swords defending the imperial banner fluttering in strange, agitated contortions in the wind." This recalls the battle scenes painted by Leonardo, Giulio Roman, and perhaps Pordenone. Titian's painting set a standard which was, according to Ridolfi, " followed by every student, " and its near Baroque impetuosity of action caused it to become a model for battle scenes painted in the 17th century.

In 1536 Federigo Gonzaga commissioned Titian to paint portrait busts of twelve Roman emperors for the Hall of Troy in his palace in Mantua, whose decoration Giulio Romano was bringing to completion. In April, 1537, the bust of Augustus was completed, followed by three others in September. However, in 1538 the last picture of the series had to be painted by Giulio Romano. The twelve paintings of figures, three-quarter length, dressed in bizarre armor, antique breast plates and royal robes, adorned with various ornaments, crests, crowns of laurel are now lost; but they soon became famous and widely known through Sadeler's engravings, Bernardino Campi's copies made in 1562 (now in the Naples Museum), as well as those of Agostino Caracci and countless other painters. Their donation, in 1628, by Vincenzo Gonzaga to Nys, who took them to England, aroused the wrath of the Mantovans. These twelve very famous pictures, supposedly inspired by antiquities in the Bembo collection and painted by Titian from medallions or antique marble sculptures, according to Dolce were acquired by Charles I. After his death they were given to the Spanish ambassador who took them home in 1652. Their history after this year is not known. Granting the alterations made in the extant engravings of the imperial portraits, still it is clear that Titian kept in mind the nature of the architecture which they were to decorate. This would partly explain the exaggerated effect of the pictures and their compliance with Giulio Romano's style of architecture, for he was the architect of Gonzaga's palace in Mantua.

Among the lost paintings traceable through extant engravings is the *Annunciation* which Titian painted for the nuns of Santa Maria degli Angeli at Murano. Unable to pay the price demanded of 500 *scudi*, they had to refuse it and turned instead to the less expensive artist, Pordenone. Following the advice of Aretino who was never lacking in ideas, Titian sent this painting to the empress who paid him 2000 *scudi*. Caraglio's engraving of this painting shows that it was a highly dramatic composition, consisting of a group of angels surrounding the dove of the Holy Spirit shedding an intense light on the Virgin who hearkens to the angel's words. Titian returned to the subject of the *Annunciation* in the large canvas which the jurist, Amelio Cortona, donated to the Scuola di San Rocco in 1555. The painting was probably executed with the help of assistants, probably shortly before the *Ecce Homo* of 1543 in Vienna. This painting shows the Angel in flight appearing to the Madonna against the background of a colonnade, a balustrade, and a peaceful landscape. It set a pattern for 16th century painters, especially Veronese.

* * *

When the Marquis d'Avalos was sent to Venice in 1539 by Charles V for the election of the Doge Pietro Lando, he may have availed himself of the opportunity to have Titian paint his portrait showing him in the act of haranguing his soldiers. This work, the *Allocution* in the Prado (Plate 21), was not begun until 1540. To compensate his client for the usual delay in delivery of the portrait, Titian informed d'Avalos through Aretino, on December 22, 1540, that he was sending him a small study, now lost, of the painting to Milan where the Marquis was staying in August, 1541. Alfonso d'Avalos is shown next to his son Ferrante who holds his helmet, standing on a pedestal in the act of rallying his soldiers. The composition is concise and closed. So is the gesturing condottiere clad in shining armor who stands out impressively against the crowd of soldiers filling the entire battle-ground with lances reaching into the sky of sunset. This is the sort of military subject which made history through Titian's concise interpretation, its essential, compositional elements serving as inspiration for Velazquez.

When Giorgio Vasari visited Venice in 1541 to work for the Cornaro family, he was commissioned by the canons of Santo Spirito in Isola to paint pictures for the ceiling of their church. After his sudden departure in August, 1542, the assignment was given to Titian, probably through the intervention of a member of the so-called Triumverate (Aretino, Titian, and Sansovino) and most likely Sansovino, who supervised the construction of the church. Paintings of the *Sacrifice of Abraham*, *The Murder of Abel*, and *David and Goliath* were finished and in place in 1544, but were transferred to Santa Maria della Salute in 1656 when the church of Santo Spirito was demolished. In this year Titian turned to Cardinal Farnese for assistance in a controversy with the monks of Santo Spirito, involving a *Descent of the Holy Ghost* which was subsequently replaced by another painting. The three paintings, now in Santa Maria della Salute, show the plastic modelling, violent forms, and agitated movement of the Mannerist style which Titian used for the first time although it had been current in Venice for some time. Mannerism, or " Raphaelism " had spread to Venice through Raphael's fame and through the work of his pupils, namely, Giulio Romano, who worked in Mantua and helped to spread the rhetorical and powerful forms of Mannerism. Titian's frequent visits to the Gonzaga court makes it certain that he must have known Giulio Romano personally. At the court Titian surely became acquainted with the refined, linear elegance of Primaticcio. The style of another Mannerist artist, Parmigianino, reached Venice in the form of engravings and countless drawings, but Parmigianino is also known to have been in Bologna in 1530 to paint the portrait of Charles V. Moreover, Mannerism in Venetian art was widespread through Francesco Salviati, called to Venice in 1539 by Grimani, and through his pupil Giuseppe Porta. Michelangelo's powerful personality had impressed the Venetians during his visit to their city. Finally, the impact of Mannerism was strengthened by Vasari's arrival in Venice in 1541 and by his companions, who had been invited by Aretino and the Compagnia della Calza for a performance of *Talanta*. Well aware though Titian was of this new movement he made few concessions to the prevailing Mannerism; he had not relinquished his personal style, especially since his conception of color could not in any way be reconciled with that of the Mannerists. A characteristic example of Titian's style at this time is the *Crowning with Thorns* (Louvre), painted for the Chapel of the Holy Crown in Santa Maria delle Grazie, Milan, whose frescoes were painted by Gaudenzio Ferrari in 1542. The strongly sculptural and violent rhythms of this painting

Fig. 20. *Venus and Adonis*. Madrid, Prado.

enhance its realistic expressionism, while the emphatic realism of some parts recalls certain tendencies in Northern Renaissance art.

In 1543 Titian signed and dated the large *Ecce Homo,* now in the Kunsthistorisches Museum, Vienna after numerous changes of ownership. This work, commissioned by the Flemish merchant Giovanni d'Anna, recalls the *Presentation in the Temple* in some aspects of its intricate architectural background. The convulsive movement of the crowd, herded together on the steps, is directed toward the figure of Christ who appears isolated and nearly lost in profound sorrow. Tradition has it that the persons depicted include Aretino, Charles V, and the Turk Suleiman, and it has been suggested that the white-robed girl in the center may be the artist's daughter Lavinia.

Another painting of this period is the *Saint John the Baptist,* originally in Santa Maria della Salute and now in the Academy, Venice (Plate 22), a splendid anatomical study of the athletic saint whose posture resembles the sculpture of Sansovino. Another work

36

Fig. 21. *Diana and Actaeon*. London, Earl of Harewood Collection.

of these years is the *Tobias and the Angel* in the church of San Marziale, Venice. Vasari says it was painted in 1507, confusing it no doubt with another version of the same subject formerly in the church of Santa Caterina and now in the Academy, Venice. However, the style of the version in San Marziale, quite different from the works of 1507 for the Fondaco dei Tedeschi, indicates that it belongs to the early 1540's. The same may be said of *Saint John the Almsgiver*, in San Giovanni Elemosinario, Venice, which was once believed to have been painted in 1533 because the date had been misread. In any event, neither painting can be counted among the artist's superior achievements.

Ridolfi observed that Titian's *Battle of Cadore* had put to shame the critics who considered Titian primarily a portraitist and those who were ignorant of his universal genius. Titian's portraits were famous because he had made extraordinary developments in this genre. In fact this was a period in which his portraits greatly outnumbered his paintings of sacred and profane subjects; but this is not the place to list them all.

37

There seems to have been no communication between Pietro Bembo and Titian after 1513, when the painter refused an invitation to come to Rome, until May 20, 1540, the date of Bembo's letter to Gerolamo Querini regarding the receipt of his " second portrait" by Titian. There are two portraits of *Pietro Bembo* of which the one in the National Gallery, Washington may well date ca. 1540, while the other in Naples, in a greatly deteriorated condition, would seem to have been painted much later, probably shortly before the cardinal's death in 1547.

No person of rank living in or passing through Venice failed to sit for Titian. In 1539 Don Diego Mendoza succeeded Lope de Soria as the ambassador of Charles V, and according to Vasari had his portrait painted by Titian in 1541. The *Portrait of Don Diego Mendoza*, now in the Pitti Gallery (Figure 14) shows the imperial envoy standing before a classical relief in a stance that prefigures the portraits of Philip II in the Prado and in Naples (Plate 27) but is reminiscent of the *Duke of Urbino* in spatial conception.

One of Titian's most delightful portraits is the *Clarice Strozzi*, signed and dated 1542 and now at the Berlin Museum (Figure 16). There is little aura of court life in the portrait, for Titian has caught instead an expression of innocence in the little girl, seemingly weary of posing for the painter who shows her leaning toward her little dog and feeding him a pretzel. This painting, adopted as a model for portraits of children by van Dyck, Velazquez and many others, still remains unsurpassed in its excellence. We tend to agree with Aretino's words of July 6, 1542, commending the artist for his work: " If I were a painter I would be heartbroken before this painting; clearly, for such a miracle Titian's brush had to await the maturity of his old age. "

In 1542 the eleven year old Ranuccio Farnese, son of Pier Luigi and nephew of Paul III, arrived in Venice to become prior of San Giovanni dei Templari. In the summer of the same year Titian painted his portrait, now in the National Gallery, Washington, a masterpiece for its candid liveliness of expression. Great admiration of the picture induced the Farnese family to obtain the artist's work for the papal court, following Aretino's repeated reproaches to the court for ignoring the master's art.

Relations between Titian and the Farnese family became much closer when Paul III decided to travel north to the region of Emilia in April, 1543, for a meeting with Charles V. While the two great men met at Busseto, near Cremona, and Titian enjoyed the hospitality of Cardinal Farnese, he painted the *Portrait of Paul III* now in the Capo di Monte Gallery, Naples, and he was paid two gold ducats for it on May 27, 1543. As a further reward the Pope offered the artist the office of Keeper of the Seal — then held by Titian's friend, the painter Sebastiano del Piombo — an honor which Titian declined in order not to hurt his friend. In the painting the Pope is represented in three-quarter view bent with age and seated in an armchair. The hollowed features of his face are rendered with rapid brushstrokes of intense color, his eyes and his bony, restless hands reflecting the magnetic power of an authoritative personality.

In 1545 Titian painted the marvelous *Portrait of Aretino* now in the Pitti Palace (Figure 19), which Aretino himself sent to Cosimo de' Medici. As Franco di Benvenuto put it in one of his sonnets, the artist conceived "within a small picture's space all the infamy of our age. " Silk and brocade clothe the figure, and the head of the famous scandal-

Fig. 22. *Rape of Europa*. Boston, Isabella Stewart Gardner Museum.

monger reveals his violent, crafty temperament in the defiant attitude which had characterized his entire life.

The style of a number of other portraits indicates their execution in the five-year period 1540 to 1545: *Doge Gritti*, one version in the Allen collection in Kenosha, another in the National Gallery, Washington, and a later third in the Czernin Collection, Vienna; *Monseigneur d'Aramont* (Castello Sforzesco, Milan), painted between 1541-1543 during the ambassador's stay in Venice; *Daniele Barbaro* (Ottawa Museum), and, that masterpiece of psychological refinement, the so-called *Young Englishman* in the Pitti Palace (Plate 23), known also as the " Gentleman with haunting eyes. " Even though variously identified as Howard, Duke of Norfolk, or Guidobaldo of Urbino, or the jurist, Ippolito Riminaldi, the man depicted here is unknown and probably will remain so forever. Still, the penetrating, pensive look of his eyes will continue to haunt the memories of anyone who has stood before this marvelous painting.

Responding to the repeated requests of the Farnese family for whom he had done a number of portraits, Titian finally decided to travel to Rome. After brief stops at the court of Guidobaldo II in Pesaro and Urbino, he arrived in Rome in early October, 1545. Greeted with honors by Pietro Bembo, Cardinal Farnese, and Paul III, as Bembo reported to Querini on October 10, Titian had " every reason to be pleased with his decision because of the abundance of beautiful antique monuments which astounded him greatly. " While staying at the Belvedere palace in the Vatican, Titian was visited by the aging Michelangelo, guided past the art treasures of Rome by Vasari, and conducted through the halls of the Vatican by Sebastiano del Piombo. Rome must have made a profound impression on Titian.

In Rome he painted another portrait of Paul III, this time at greater leisure, showing the Pope in full length reclining in an armchair in the company of his nephews, Ottavio and Alessandro Farnese. The impressive canvas is now in the Capodimonte Gallery in Naples (Plates 24 and 25). This work introduced a new type of portrait, one which includes several figures in reciprocal, emotional contact, a form that may be called a " profane conversation " as distinct from the " sacred conversation " in altarpieces. Its broad pictorial effect of animated brushstrokes, color patches and the sketchiness of some parts foreshadows Titian's late style. The composition is entirely devoid of formal conventions; instead it captures a fleeting moment, in the personal response of the Pope and his nephews.

While in Rome Titian completed the *Danae*, one of his most perfectly balanced and successful mythological creations, now in the Capodimonte Gallery (Plate 19). Vasari saw the picture in the company of Michelangelo who " praised it greatly " but added (if we are to believe Vasari's words), " it is a pity that the art of drawing is not being taught well in Venice. " The *Danae* is remarkable for the originality of its conception, the magnificent nude being portrayed in a new, rhythmic movement. It is the prototype of other versions of this subject executed about ten years later, such as those in the Kunsthistorisches Museum, Vienna, the Prado, and the Hermitage, Leningrad.

Other pictures painted by Titian for the Farnese and now lost are the *Ecce Homo*, a double portrait of Paul III and his son Pier Luigi, and one of Margaret of Parma, the wife of Ottavio Farnese. In Rome Titian painted for Guidobaldo II of Urbino two portraits of members of the Della Rovere family who had been popes and were now dead. For the one of Julius II (Pitti Palace) he worked from Raphael's famous original once in Santa Maria del Popolo and now lost; for that of Sixtus IV (Uffizi) he used a medallion painted by Melozzo da Forli in the fresco decoration of the Vatican. In March, 1546, when his sojourn in the papal city was drawing to a close, Roman citizenship was conferred on Titian. During his return journey to Venice he stayed briefly in Florence where he visited Cosimo de' Medici in his villa at Poggio a Cajano, and offered to paint his portrait. On June 19, of the same year Titian was home again.

In Venice once again, Titian completed the altarpiece of the *Madonna with Saints Peter and Paul*, begun in 1542 for the Cathedral of Serravalle and originally commissioned

Fig. 23. *The Descent of the Holy Spirit*. Venice, Santa Maria della Salute.

Fig. 24. *Martyrdom of Saint Lawrence*. Venice, Santa Maria dei Gesuiti.

Fig. 25. *Saint Sebastian*. Leningrad, Hermitage.

to his brother Francesco. It is a rather poor work, done with the extensive help of work-shop assistants. The *Saint James of Compostello* in the church of San Lio is another work of this period. In these years portrait painting took up most of the artist's time. It may have been shortly before his departure for Augsburg that he painted the *Votive Portrait of the Vendramin Family* in the National Gallery, London (Plate 26 and Figure 18), one of his greatest achievements in this field. Members of the family kneel in prayer before an altar containing the Holy Cross between two flaming candles, a motif which El Greco was to adopt. The event takes place outdoors, under a cloud-filled, blue sky, and the Vendramin family is rhythmically grouped in a variety of poses, making a lively interplay of forms and movement. The new energy of the composition may perhaps owe something to Raphael's *Mass of Bolsena* in the Vatican. Spatial depth in the scene is enhanced by the position of the children in groups of three on either side, as well as the color vibrations marked by rich, red tones.

42

In January, 1548, Titian left Venice for Augsburg at the request of Charles V. He was accompanied by his son Orazio, his nephew Cesare Vecellio, and his pupil Lambert Sustris. As an homage to be offered to the emperor he took along an *Ecce Homo* (probably the one now in the Prado) of which he left behind a copy for Aretino.

In Augsburg he immediately prepared for work, ready to portray the illustrious members of the Diet and above all its convocator, Charles V himself. In April, 1548, he had already begun the magnificent painting, *Charles V on Horseback* (Figure 17) now in the Prado, a masterpiece of equestrian portraiture. In adopting this form, an ancient iconographic motif, Titian endowed it with a new interpretation, both as regards a vital strength and hieratic solemnity. Charles V is shown on horseback in a landscape, departing for the victorious battle of Mühlberg. The horse quivers with barely restrained ardor as he begins to trot away. Firmly seated, implacable in his austere imperial dignity, the Emperor stands out not only physically but also as an embodiment of supreme temporal power. The painting inspired many a 17th century artist, among them Rubens, van Dyck, and Velazquez. While in Augsburg, Titian painted another portrait of Charles V seated in a loggia (Munich Museum). The mood of this painting is one of simplicity and human warmth. Charles V is dressed simply, without ostentatious splendor, and the expression in his eyes seems dimmed by melancholy thoughts.

Among the many portraits painted by Titian in these years we may mention that of the wife of Charles V, *Isabella of Portugal* (Prado); the double portrait, now lost, of the imperial couple (of which there exists a copy by Rubens); the portrait of the *Grand Elector, John Frederick of Saxony* whom Charles V had taken prisoner (Kunsthistorisches Museum, Vienna); the portrait of the chancellor *Nicola Perrenot di Granvelle* (Besançon) and that of his son *Antonio Perrenot* (Nelson Art Gallery, Kansas City). All are works of great formal perfection and some reveal the influence of German painters such as Cranach and Holbein. Titian also portrayed the sister of Charles V, Queen Mary of Hungary; Christine of Denmark; Maria Giacomina of Baden; Maurice of Saxony; Dorothea, Countess Palatine; Maximilian, King of Bohemia; Emanuele Filiberto of Savoy; King Ferdinand I; the Archduke Ferdinand; and the Duke of Alba, — all of whom attended the Diet at Augsburg. Many of these portraits have been lost.

Such a number of works done in a relatively short time (and while working on others) reveals Titian's extraordinary swiftness of execution and his rare gift of grasping the essential aspects of his sitter's character. His method was to make a sketch from life and then at leisure to complete the portrait in his studio. The *Venus with the Organist* (Plate 20) now in the Prado, was probably painted at Augsburg or shortly before his visit there, and similar versions were painted later. Having long since abandoned the ideal of classical beauty in the nude figure, in this painting Titian continues the ideal which he had formulated in the *Danae* (Plate 19), now giving sensuous aspects greater emphasis. In subsequent versions of this subject, Titian substituted a lute player for the organist and added a landscape background, as in the *Venus and the Lute Player* in the Metropolitan Museum, New York and one of slightly inferior quality in the Fitzwilliam Museum, Cambridge, both dating ca. 1560.

On his way home from Augsburg, Titian interrupted his journey to stop at Innsbruck where he painted portraits of the daughters of King Ferdinand. Late in October, 1548, after an absence of almost ten months, he was back in Venice. Here he must have gone to work immediately on paintings of the *Condemned* or *Furies* commissioned in Augsburg by Mary of Hungary, the sister of Charles V. Of the four subjects mentioned by Vasari only two are extant: *Sisyphus* and the so-called *Prometheus,* both in the Prado. Although the movement and the Mannerist foreshortening of figures in these works is reminiscent of the ceilings painted some years earlier in Santa Maria della Salute, Titian here achieved much greater pictorial and dramatic effects. Summoned again to Augsburg by the Emperor in November, 1550, Titian presented him with the *Mater Dolorosa* (Prado), which eventually accompanied Charles V into his retirement at San Juste. While in Augsburg, he also painted the portrait of *Prince Philip of Spain* (Prado), begun in January, 1551, a full-length figure wearing an elaborate suit of armor. His relations with Philip were to last all his life. While still in Augsburg, Titian painted other pictures and portraits before returning to Venice in August, 1551. The painter, now at the threshold of old age but undaunted in spirit, was not to leave Venice again.

His return home appears to have inspired Titian with new pictorial ideas and greater freedom. Even his portraits show a new spirit, less austere and pensive than those executed while in Germany. To illustrate this development it suffices to mention the more notable examples: the *Knight of Malta* (Prado); the so-called *Duke of Atri* (Kassel) (Figure 13) which anticipates the paintings of Velazquez; and the *Doge Francesco Venier* (Lugano, Thyssen collection) painted against the background of a distant fire on the lagoon. A portrait of which Philip acknowledged receipt in a letter to Titian dated June 18, 1553, may be the *Prince Philip* (Plate 27) now in Naples, a full-length figure standing out clearly and haughtily against a neutral ground rendered in delicate grey and green hues. Other portraits of this decade include those of the Archbishop *Filippo Archinto* (Metropolitan Museum, New York); *Lodovico Beccadelli,* Bishop of Ravello (Uffizi); and the *Franciscan Monk with a Book* (Melbourne). Many other portraits, for which there are documents, have been lost, among them those of Guidobaldo II (1552); Francesco Vargas, the Spanish ambassador in Venice; Titian's self-portrait which Vargas sent to Philip; the portraits of Alfonso I and Ercole II of Ferrara (1556); and many more. While engaged on these portraits of men, Titian also painted biblical and mythological subjects which emphasized feminine beauty: *Venus with a Mirror* (National Gallery, Washington); *Salome* (Prado); and the *Young Lady holding a Fruit Bowl* (Berlin Museum), a marvelous work of unsurpassed spontaneity.

In 1552 Titian had sent to Philip a *Landscape* now lost, and a *Portrait of Saint Margaret,* probably the one now in the Escorial, which recalls the compositions of Raphael. Another version was made some ten years later in the signed canvas in the Prado, a work full of poetic and somewhat dramatic accents, especially in the saint's intense expressiveness and the impressive landscape which includes a fire. Titian's relations with Spain continued without interruption. In 1553 he informed Philip of the near completion of certain " poetic subjects, " in reference to a number of mythological compositions which are consummate expressions of his poetic imagination. In the following

44

Fig. 26. *The Flaying of Marsyas.* Kromieriz, Czechoslovakia, Gallery.

year he sent Charles V the *Holy Trinity* (La Gloria), now in the Prado, which the Emperor had commissioned him to paint for his private retreat. This is an ambitious composition that is intentionally grandiose and impressive; it is inspired to some extent by Michelangelo, but aside from being very different, frankly it is not entirely successful. The most important one of the poetic subjects painted for Philip is the *Venus and Adonis* (Prado) which was sent to London in 1554 for the wedding of Philip and Mary of Tudor. Harmoniously arranged in a lively rhythm, the figures are absorbed in a landscape of elegiac

45

intensity that extends to the violence of the sky. The scene is fraught with forebodings of Adonis's imminent death which Venus tries in vain to prevent. The subject was so successful that Titian returned to it repeatedly with only slight variations. At this time, he was also making other paintings of Danae, such as the one now in the Prado, following the first version which is now in Naples (Plate 19). The new versions are not only more free but also the handling is characterized by bold strokes and color fragmentations.

In this period the artist may have painted the famous *Venus of Pardo* (Plate 28 and Figure 15), now in the Louvre, which has been variously dated. The scene actually represents " Antiope surprised by Jupiter in the disguise of a satyr. " Although the composition recalls in some respects the Bacchanalian scenes painted for the Duke of Ferrara, the pictorial vision of this picture is more free and richer in details. The large canvas summarizes Titian's development from his early Giorgionesque lyricism through moments when his genius rediscovers landscape. It is generally thought that the painting was made in the late 1530's, but its broad fluid handling seems to indicate that it was repainted at a later date. We may not be too far off in suggesting a date around 1560 for this work, as was once proposed by Fogolari and also recommended recently.

In spite of his increasingly pressing commitments to the imperial family, Titian maintained close ties with Venetian patrons. In 1555-1556 he painted a votive picture showing the Doge Marcello Trevisan kneeling before the Virgin and saints for the Ducal Palace, where it perished in the great fire of 1575. For the church of Santa Maria Nuova in Venice he painted the altarpiece of *Saint Jerome* (Brera, Milan), a subject he had chosen several years earlier for the canvas now in the Louvre, conceived in a new color range, shifting from russet to umber tones in near monochrome. Shortly before 1559, a dramatic painting of the *Martyrdom of Saint Lawrence* (Figure 24) was installed in the Church of the Crociferi (later of the Jesuits). Vasari praises it very much. Though commissioned as early as 1548 by Lorenzo Massolo, the painting was not completed at the patron's death in 1557, and actually was not finished until two years later. Titian must have thought about the subject a long time, and experienced it deeply. It is difficult to determine now whether he was stirred by the remembrance of Raphael's *Fire In The Borgo*, in the Vatican, or by the work of Mannerists, or by Michelangelo himself. Conceived in violent contrasts of light flashing over the agitated crowd and on buildings, this painting may be considered a forerunner of Tintoretto's late paintings in the handling of light. These were years of feverish creative activity. In 1558 the altarpiece representing the *Crucifixion with the Virgin, Saints Dominic and John* was installed in the church of Saint Dominic, Ancona. To the same period we may ascribe the brilliant *Annunciation* in the church of Saint Dominic, Naples, as well as the solemn though somewhat conventional *Descent of the Holy Spirit* in Santa Maria della Salute (Figure 23).

During the years 1559-1562, Titian worked on many paintings for Philip II. Among mythological subjects which he had promised the King was *Perseus and Andromeda* (Wallace Collection, London). The foreshortened figure of Perseus tumbling down from the rock may have been inspired by the ideas of Tintoretto. In 1559 Titian completed two more poetic subjects for Philip, *Diana and Actaeon* and *Diana and Callisto*, both in Edinburgh. Another version of the latter is now in Vienna. The compact lucidity of

Fig. 27. *Madonna and Saints and the Artist.* Pieve di Cadore, Archbishop's Church.

Titian's early Bacchanalian scenes is a far cry from these new pictorial conceptions by Titian which foreshadow and anticipate modern movements in art.

The testimony of his biographers offers us a better understanding of the late phase of Titian's art. Already in 1557 Dolce stated that in Titian's compositions " there is a continuous interplay of light and shadow whose subtle gradations reflect corresponding changes in nature itself. " Vasari's statements are more explicit for their emphasis on the difference between Titian's mature art and that of his youth: " It is true that in his last works his way of painting is quite different from that of his youth; whereas his early works were done with incredible refinement and application, and equally impressive when seen from close-by or far away, his later works, executed in bold strokes and patches of color, are unintelligible at close range but appear perfect when seen at a distance. "

Titian's technique was treated amply in 1674 by Boschini who had been advised in these matters by Palma the Younger who had " the good fortune to enjoy the master's erudite guidance. " Boschini expresses Palma the Younger's views on Titian's technique, saying " he weighed down his canvases with masses of color sufficient to form a ground or foundation for his forms; he then superposed on, and modelled through, them. The ground thus provided, he turned the paintings to the wall without looking at them sometimes for months; when he finally took to the brush again, he scrutinized them with the careful attention he would give a formidable enemy, to see what faults he could find "; in adding the finishing touches, he " used his fingers rather than his brush. " A characteristic example of this technique gradually developed by Titian to its highest level is the poetic subject of *Diana and Actaeon* (Figure 21) from the Earl of Harewood's collection now in the National Gallery, London. The reckless shepherd, attacked by a pack of hounds, seems to merge with the bushes, shrubs and trees into a vibrant texture of crackling, brownish flames. Another, in this genre, is the *Rape of Europe* (Figure 22), which was sent to Philip II in 1562 and is now in the Gardener Museum, Boston. Here a mythological theme has been translated into a melodious composition which transcends reality as it dissolves into light effects of silver and blue.

These poetic themes were preceded by two important religious pictures painted in 1559 for the King of Spain: the *Entombment,* in the Prado (Plate 32) and the *Adoration of the Magi* in the Escorial. In the *Entombment,* Titian achieved an intensely dramatic and tragic effect by representing the body of Christ in a foreshortened, diagonal perspective. This is Titian's own innovation which harmonizes with the agitated postures of the grief-stricken figures, among which that of the Magdalene stands out conspicuously. Copies and variants of the *Entombment* exist in Vienna, in the Ambrosiana, Milan, in the Prado and elsewhere. In the *Adoration* in the Escorial, Titian gave an equally original interpretation of an old iconographic subject by introducing lively and realistic episodes in the composition. Among various versions of this painting, we may cite as authentic the ones in the Ambrosiana, the Cleveland Museum, and the Prado.

Other works of the late fifties include the votive painting of the *Doge Antonio Grimani before Faith* (Escorial), begun in 1556, but finished much later largely by assistants, and two versions of *Christ in the Garden,* one in the Escorial, the other in the Prado. Both are tragic and moving creations. These two contemporary works are expressive syntheses, especially daring in the conception of light effects, particularly the latter which anticipates Rembrandt's paintings in a nocturnal light. The admirable *Madonna with the Child* of the Pinakothek in Munich, formerly in a sacristy of the Escorial, was likewise painted around 1560.

* * *

In the early 1560's, Titian was little more than seventy years old; he had reached the height of his fame and of his indomitable creative energy. In these years he produced some of the most expressive and significant achievements in painting. His physical appearance at this time, probably reflected in the *Self-Portrait* now in Berlin, was an image of austere, aloof self-assurance. We may overlook the less important, damaged works and those predominently by his assistants, — the *Transfiguration* (Church of San Salvatore); the altarpiece of *Saint Francis with the Donor Francesco Guidone* (Ascoli Piceno); and the *Saint Nicholas of Bari* (San Sebastiano, Venice). We turn to paintings executed for Philip II to see Titian's more important achievements of that time. In 1564 he sent Philip the *Last Supper* which was trimmed at the margins when it came to the Escorial and has since been disfigured by repainting. Other paintings in the Escorial include the *Crucifixion* which recalls the version in Ancona. However, there is no trace of the

48

Fig. 28. Drawing. *The Jealous Husband.* Paris, École des Beaux-Arts.

Magdalene which the painter delivered to Philip II in 1561; the composition, so well described by Vasari, was duplicated in the *Magdalene* in the Hermitage and in many other versions. To the period 1560-1570 belongs also the *Adam and Eve* in the Prado (Plate 35), the composition of which is rather archaic but exquisitely sensitive in color and rich in tonality and musical rhythms.

The aims of Titian in this period are probably best expressed in the *Annunciation* in San Salvatore (Plates 33 and 34), painted shortly before 1566 and mentioned by Vasari, who failed, however, to appreciate its innovations and its transcendent force. A deep light of reddish tones radiates throughout the scene like a glowing shower, transfiguring the sacred episode and pervading it with a sensation of almost painful rejoicing. Truly a masterpiece of the artist's mature years! Diametrically opposed to it in subject-matter, but equally perfect in imagery, is a profane theme which was painted at this time, the joyfully classic *Education of Cupid*, now in the Borghese Gallery, Rome (Plates 29 and 30). This canvas too was executed with the rough, stippled brush work which became popular in 19th century painting, especially in Impressionism. These massive strokes of color, " in patches " as Boschini describes, seem to evoke the nature of sunlight itself to produce the intense luminosity emanating from the color-rich texture.

When in Venice from May 21 to 27, 1566, Vasari saw the following works " sketched or in an initial stage " in Titian's studio: *Christ on the Cross*, probably the fragment now in Bologna; the already mentioned *Doge Grimani before Faith* in the Ducal palace; three mythological pictures which were once in the Palazzo Civico, Brescia, all of them later destroyed by fire; *Religion Defended by Spain* (Prado); *Christ Appearing to Magdalene in the Garden;* a *The Dead Christ with the Madonna and The Three Marys;* a *Self-Portrait;* a half-length figure of *Saint Paul Reading.* Some of these are not easily identifiable today.

One of the more important works of this period is the *Martyrdom of Saint Lawrence* (Escorial). Reminiscent in its treatment of the version in the Church of the Crociferi, but lacking its architectural background, this painting is even more emotional and unreal by virtue of its nocturnal effects and provocative for its more impetuous, vehement, execution. Other significant works were three paintings formerly in Brescia: *Forge of Vulcan* of which an engraving is preserved; *Minerva, Mars and the Three Naiads; Ceres and Bacchus.* These works reached their destination two years after Vasari had seen them, but were destroyed by fire in 1575. The authorities in Brescia questioned the authenticity of these works. Although they may have been executed in part by assistants, they were viewed with suspicion probably because there was little understanding at this time of Titian's old-age style. One of the most significant works of this period is *Religion Defended by Spain* (Plate 36). Vasari described it as " a nude girl bowing to Minerva accompanied by another figure, and the sea with Neptune on a carriage in the background, " thus indicating his inability to interpret correctly the meaning of this allegory. Titian, who had originally intended the picture for Alfonso d'Este, later repainted it completely (as was his custom) transforming it into a symphony of colors that glow beneath a seemingly veiled surface.

In October, 1568, the painter informed Philip II that he had completed the *Christ*

50

Fig. 29. Drawing. *Portrait of a Woman.* Florence, Uffizi.

Fig. 30. Drawing. *Studies for the Saint Sebastian in Brescia.* Berlin, Kupferstichkabinett.

Fig. 31. Drawing. *Study for the Saint Sebastian in Brescia.* Frankfurt, Städelsches Institut.

and the Pharisee (National Gallery, London), a painting closely suggesting certain effects in the paintings of Caravaggio. In the same year he offered Maximilan II seven mythological paintings now lost or at least no longer identifiable. The themes of these paintings corresponded to those previously executed for Philip II. Another work of these years is the *Christ Carrying the Cross* repeated later in other versions, resuming a subject he had painted in his youth for the Scuola di San Rocco and which he now endows with greater pathos.

In 1565 Titian went to Pieve di Cadore to attend to frescoes in the Archbishop's Church, the execution of which is the work of his pupils, Cesare Vecellio, Emanuele di Augusta, Valerio Zuccato and others, following drawings made by the master in 1567. These murals perished when the building was demolished in 1813. It may have been on this occasion that he donated to the church in his native village the *Madonna with St. Andrew, San Tiziano and the Artist* (Figure 27), a work once attributed to his pupils but now accepted as by his own hand. Titian's self-portrait in this votive painting is profoundly spiritual. The image of the Madonna and Child is one of the oldest iconographic motifs in Venetian art, which Titian has conceived with all its feeling of tenderness and resignation. Closely resembling this work and probably done only a few years later is the *Madonna and the Nursing Child* (formerly, Mond collection; now National Gallery, London). Unanimously accepted as one of the aged Titian's masterpieces, this was painted in silvery tones bathed in subdued light.

Fully preoccupied with important commissions for palaces and churches, Titian

52

found less time now for portraiture to which he had devoted so much attention in the past. Among the few portraits painted after 1560 are two which are signed and dated 1561: *Man with the Palm* (Dresden), allegedly representing Antonio Palma called Palma Vecchio, the father of Palma the Younger; *Gentleman with a Book* (Walters Art Gallery, Baltimore). About this time Titian may have painted the *Portrait of a Man with a Flute* (Detroit Institute of Arts) and the portrait of his daughter, *Lavinia* (Dresden) identified through an inscription. Belonging stylistically to this period is the superb *Self-Portrait* (Berlin), which may be the one seen by Vasari in the painter's studio. However, Titian's most outstanding portrait is the antiquarian, *Jacopo Strada*, in Vienna (Plate 31), dated 1566 and appropriately defined by an art critic as the " picture of a profession. " The man is shown offering a statuette of Venus to an imaginary customer; on the table are antique coins and a letter, and two precious books are placed on top of a cabinet. The portrait recalls those painted by Lorenzo Lotto which must have been known to Titian.

In the last decade of his life which came to an end in 1576, Titian, now over eighty years old, still had the strength to create a number of outstanding masterpieces. In August, 1571, he announced to Philip II the despatch of *Roman Lucretia Raped by Tarquinius* (Fitzwilliam Museum, Cambridge), a picture which teems with plastic and painterly vitality. The episode is rendered with dramatic violence, the figures dominating the space in their growing passion. The *Tarquinius and Lucrezia* in the Academy, Vienna, (Plate 38), was painted slightly later. Here the episode is conceived in greater pictorial synthesis, the gestures less theatrical, the drama giving way to an intense expressionism that is manifest in a symphony of ripe colors in full bloom. Dvořak described the effect as " blumige Farben " when he published an article on this masterpiece which is so amazingly modern.

The aged Titian's " poetry in color " comes forth in all its drama and revolutionary power if we compare *The Crowning with Thorns* in Munich with *The Crowning with Thorns* in the Louvre, painted in the 1540's. Although his grouping of figures is almost identical in both pictures, the painterly difference is such that the Louvre version (certainly a work of the early seventies) hardly reminds us of his conception of thirty years earlier. The scene has become a nocturnal tragedy, placed amid flickering flames and eerie phantoms. It seems almost an act of predestination that this work wound up in the hands of Tintoretto during the disposal of Titian's estate. Equally dramatic in its approach is the *Ecce Homo* in the Saint Louis Museum. Its conception foreshadows the work of Rembrandt in its effect of contrasting lights as well as in the use of a man dressed as an oriental wearing a fur hat adorned with pearls. There is also the powerful *Saint Sebastian* in the Hermitage, Leningrad (Figure 25), modelled with daubs and patches of color and radiating a warm luminosity against a ground whose vehement brushstrokes writhe as if in a vortex. This painting may truly be said to have shaken art from its very foundation.

The *Flaying of Marsyas* in the Kremsier Gallery (Kromieriz, Czechoslovakia) (Figure 26) is, in my opinion, the most tragic and painful of Titian's last paintings. This mythological tale is literally like a funerary pyre which sends forth sparks and smoke. The picture itself seems to have caught fire, consumed as it were in a final surge of flames.

This moment in Titian's life is followed by an interlude of surprising, spiritual tranquility. As if soothed by memories of the past, he painted a pastoral theme as poetic, peaceful, and bucolic as the *Shepherd and Nymph* in Vienna (Plate 37). Here is a last homage to feminine beauty that is filled with lingering echoes of the Giorgionesque past, and yet transformed by his new pictorial language.

To the end of his life the painter tried to satisfy the wishes of Philip, King of Spain. Shortly after sending him *Roman Lucrezia Raped by Tarquinius*, he was commissioned a painting commemorating the battle of Lepanto (1571). In this painting in the Prado (*Allegory of the Battle of Lepanto*), Philip II offers his new born son, the Infante Don Fernando to Victory. The painting, begun in 1573, and shipped to Spain in 1575, is one of Titian's last documented works. Though exalting the spirit of victory, the painting is fraught with sadness and even impending death. Against the light of flames engulfing the doomed Turkish fleet, the King raises his son toward the image of Victory hurtling down from above with a violence that is reminiscent of Tintoretto but comparable to Titian's painting of *Perseus and Andromeda* (Wallace Collection). The prisoner at the monarch's feet may have been added by Vincente Carducho in 1625 when documents state that he was commissioned and paid to enlarge and restore the canvas. Although the painting is not in its original condition, it is doubtful that the prisoner was created by the Spanish restorer; rather he may simply have repainted Titian's original. On the other hand, the deformed feet of Victory are clearly due to the incompetent brush of the restorer.

The extensive correspondence between Titian and Philip II over the years became more exacting during the painter's last years. As if troubled by the destiny of death, Titian pressed Philip for payment of many paintings furnished him. In a moving letter written in 1571, pointing out his own misery and appealing to the King's grace, Titian mentions his old age, claiming, perhaps in good faith, to be ninety-five years old, whereas in fact he was about age eighty-three. Renewing his appeals in 1574, at Christmas, 1576, and finally in February, 1576, a few months before his death, Titian, conscious of his own greatness, urges the monarch to " act in accordance with my reputation as an honorable gentleman held in great esteem by the world. " Feeling his end near, Titian asked to be buried in the Church of the Frari, where his *Assumption* had marked the start of his fame and fortune. To this purpose he promised the Franciscans of the church a large *Pietà* (Plates 39 and 40). However, disagreement with the monks induced him to suspend the work, which was unfinished when he died on August 27, 1576. He was buried in the Church of the Frari on the following day; and though a plague raged unabated, he was honored with solemn funeral rites worthy of the prince of painting.

The *Pietà* was finished by Palma the Younger, and installed in the church of Sant' Angelo, until demolition of the church caused it to be housed in the Academy, Venice. Recent investigations of the color structure have revealed Palma's contribution to be rather insignificant; thus, it may be accepted as Titian's last painting. Its dramatic rhythm culminates in the powerful figure of the Magdalene, who rushes forward in anguish and uncontrolled grief. A portal-like niche of rough-hewn stones forms an apse decorated with glistening mosaic, the central motif of which is a pelican symbolizing resurrection.

54

Fig. 32. Drawing. *Jupiter and Io*. Cambridge, Fitzwilliam Museum.

Statues to the right and left of the niche represent Moses and Faith. Before the niche is the dead Christ resting in his Mother's arms, while Joseph of Arimathea kneels at His feet. A votive plaque representing Titian and his son Orazio praying to the Virgin may be seen in the lower right-hand corner, under the lion's head decorating the pedestal of Faith. The little plaque is like a humble prayer inserted in the greater one, the Pietà itself, bold and grandiose in style, an artistic and spiritual testament left by Titian to his successors.

*   *   *

In quantity alone, the masterpieces created by Titian in slightly more than seventy years surpass those by artists whose œuvre is extensive, namely Rubens, Rembrandt, and Goya. However, the unique aspects of Titian's creative spirit are his continuous development in expressive form, from the earliest paintings of 1505-1507 to the one painted in the year of his death in 1576, and an equally continuous transformation of his pictorial means. His genius burst forth in a vigorous manifestation of unbelievable precocity, and continued to assert itself in an unceasing obsession with perfection to his very end.

Any effort to divide Titian's œuvre into neat periods is purely arbitrary, and it serves merely practical purposes for scholarly classification. I have separated the artist's work into three periods, but this could easily be revised to suit any didactic purpose. In reality there were no breaks in his work, no sudden changes in direction. New ideas evolved out of new contacts, fresh outlooks and insights in various fields, resumption of themes conceived in his youth, and reinterpretation of subjects from a different point of view. And yet these never resulted in an abrupt change, nor did they break the continuity of his œuvre. The artist's vision of the world was never at variance with his own individual personality. Even the so-called Mannerist crisis emphasized by recent art-criticism, affected Titian's work merely to the extent that he might occasionally borrow from Michelangelo an idea or suggestion that had particular significance. Little indeed did the Mannerist elements of Franco, Salviati, Vasari, and Michelangelo's followers mean to a Titian. True, a few ideas of Raphael and some formal concepts of his pupil Giulio Romano made a momentary impression on Titian. Inherent in his pictorial means there was an extraordinary richness of chords, melodies, tonalities, and nuances. There is the lyricism of the *Fête Champêtre*, the dramatic in the Padua murals, the epic prose of history in the lost *Battle of Cadore* and the *Allocution of Alfonso d'Avalos;* secular and sacred allegories in *The Trinity* (*La Gloria*) and the *Allegory of the Battle of Lepanto*. In short Titian moved freely into, and became a sovereign in, every realm of art. His instinctive feelings for nature alternates, or rather coexists, with a deep-seated sensitivity to religion in the most profound sense of the word. It may be because of his true religiousness that Titian's art probed the essence of life, penetrating the recesses whose forms can not be seen by human eyes; rather they are experienced and are transformed into sensations of a metaphysical nature, as is the case in his more mature creations.

To summarize the division of the artist's work into three periods, — the first shows him refining Giorgione's concepts, especially his vivid sense of color, in a direct confrontation with nature. Titian created a new standard of Greek beauty in representing the human figure, giving it greater substance, lifelike in warm, delicate colors, so different from Giorgione's linear style, and creating a full-bodied, elegiac synthesis. To these ends he employed an impasto of color that is fluid and broad in the sustained vibration of sensitive, delicate strokes. A lively vision of the real world was dawning upon a youthful mind, who discovered and grasped it in paintings of marvelous quality.

In his middle period (roughly from 1520 to 1545), Titian deepened the concepts and inspiration of paintings made in his youth. Now he is less hedonistic, more inclined to extract the essential and timeless aspects of the human figure, and endowing it with new dignity. His color continues to be vibrant, but it is thicker, its tonality deeper, sometimes ember-like and frequently near monochrome. This he achieved through a new technique,

56

judging from Boschini's comments regarding Titian's mature style, which was emulated in later centuries and has its ideal equivalent in Michelangelo's style of forms unfinished. The lyrical phase gave way almost imperceptibly to a more somber view and an awareness of life's tragic seriousness. This coincides with the spirit of the Counter Reformation and with the religious motives of the Council of Trent in 1545.

In Titian's last period, the premonitions of a world in change were felt even more acutely. He tackles and synthesizes with the boldest experiments ever undertaken in painting, not in pursuit of an aesthetic for its own sake, but because of the urge for a personal language with which to give his art expressive imagery. Visions evoked by a mind now conceived with a transcendented world of eternity, Titian's figures of his last years are no longer tangible creatures but immanent apparitions of sublime, moral significance, stripped of unessential details as if immersed in the flaming atmosphere of another cosmos.

The language of the now solitary, aging genius was not understood by his contemporaries. Some men, like the antiquarian Stoppo writing to Fugger in 1568, ascribed his faulty painting to failing eyesight and trembling hands; recently other critics have imputed his broken color and his unfinished forms to his farsightedness of vision, and his impetuous application of color to arthritis. But this way of painting is already noticeable ca. 1540 and was developed in full in the *Portrait of Paul III and his Nephews* of 1545 (Plates 24 and 25). Titian was then between fifty and sixty years old; arthritis and deterioration of vision were still a long way off. These so-called explanations of the creative process through physical defects (be they opthalmic or circulatory) bring to mind the opinions of art critics in the early 20th century who undertook to prove that El Greco's elongated figures were the result of his astigmatism. The truth is that Titian conceived the unfocused, unfinished forms, separated as they were from precision in drawing and tactile values, in order to transform visual reality into a timeless, supremely ideal world. Through this pictorial language alone — unique in its time — Titian expressed himself fully and without restraint.

ANTONIO MORASSI

NOTES
on illustrations for the text

Fig. 1
SLEEPING VENUS. Canvas, 42¹/₂ x 69 in. (108 x 175 cm.) Dresden, Gallery.

Acquired by August of Saxony from the French art dealer Ch. Le Roy in 1697 as a work by Giorgione and so listed in the catalogue of the Royal Gallery in 1707, the painting was mentioned later as a work by Titian (Catalogue of 1772, etc.). In the 19th century the picture, initially (1856) considered a copy of a Titian by Sassoferrato, was reattributed to Giorgione, until Morelli (1880) suggested it might be the painting which Michiel saw in Gerolamo Marcello's house in 1526 and described by Michiel as a " picture of a nude Venus sleeping in a landscape with a Cupid, by the hand of Zorzo de Castelfranco, but the landscape and Cupid finished by Titian. "

During the painting's restoration in 1843, the figure of Cupid was discovered under an overlay of paint, and it was later painted out again (see Gamba, 1928-29 and Posse, 1931); this discovery seems to confirm Morelli's hypothesis. Yet Titian's contribution obviously was not confined to the landscape and the Cupid. The Venus herself, even though conceived in Giorgione's linear, poetic manner, is indicative in parts of Titian's broad, powerful style.

Fig. 2
MADONNA WITH THE CHILD AND SAINTS ROCH AND ANTHONY. Canvas, 36¹/₄ x 52¹/₄ in. (92 x 133 cm.) Madrid, Prado.

The picture was offered to Philip IV of Spain by the Viceroy of Naples, Duke of Medina, and mentioned a few years later by Santos (1657) as being in the sacristy of the Escorial " by the hand of Bordonon " (to whom Velazquez also attributed the work). The painting came to the Prado in 1936.

The painting has been attributed to Pordenone, to Francesco Vecellio (Cavalcaselle), to Domenico Campagnola (von Hadeln), and to Giorgione (Morelli). The latter attribution is being maintained by some scholars. It was rightly attributed to Titian by Schmidt in 1908, and is today so accepted by nearly every critic. A work to be dated prior to the Padua murals.

Fig. 3
SACRED CONVERSATION OF CASA BALBI. Canvas, 51 x 65 in. (130 x 185 cm.) Genoa, Palazzo Balbi-Piovera.

The painting showing the Madonna and Child with Saint Catherine, Dominic and a donor was mentioned as a work of Titian by Ratti (*Istruzione su quanto può vedersi di più bello a Genova*, 1780, 187) and by Alizeri (*Guida artistica*, 1847, II, 75); it may have come from the Venetian branch of the Balbi family.

This work was unknown until 1946, even though mentioned previously by Cavalcaselle as one contemporary with the Bacchanalian scenes. It was published and

added to Titian's œuvre by Morassi as one of the masterpieces of his early period.

Fig. 4
So-called PORTRAIT OF ARIOSTO. Canvas, 32 x 26 in. (81.2 x 66.3 cm.) London, National Gallery.

The letters T...V... are inscribed on the parapet.

An engraving by Persijn after a drawing by Sandrart shows the original to have been in the collection of Alfonso Lopez, counselor of the King of Spain, which included the *Flora* now at the Uffizi. An inventory of paintings owned by Van Dyck (1644) mentioned a *Poet Ariosto* by Titian, probably the picture now in London. Owned successively by Lord Darnley and Sir Donaldson (1904), the painting finally came to the National Gallery where it was catalogued as a portrait of *Ariosto*. But the physiognomy of the man does not resemble that properly known as the poet's. Equally unsubstantiated is the hypothetical identification as the portrait of the nobleman of Casa Barbarigo, mentioned by Vasari and allegedly painted by Titian around 1506, which " but for the indication of Vecellio's name would have been considered a work of Giorgione. "

Fig. 5
NOLI ME TANGERE. Canvas, 42³/₄ x 35¹/₄ in. (109 x 90 cm.) London, National Gallery.

Identifiable as the *Magdalene with Christ in the Garden* which Ridolfi (1648) mentioned as a work by Titian in the Collection of Cristoforo and Francesco Muselli in Verona. Acquired by the Marquis de Seignelay (d. 1690), the painting subsequently formed part of the collection of Pierre Vincent Bertin (d. 1711), was listed in the catalogue of the gallery of the Duke of Orleans in 1727, and sold to the banker Walkuers in 1792. It was brought to England by Laborde de Méréville, and after further changes in ownership finally came to the National Gallery in 1856 as part of the Rogers bequest.

Accepted unanimously as a work of the younger Titian (in spite of the unfounded suggestion that it might be only the finished version by Titian of a subject originally begun by Giorgione), the *Noli Me Tangere* must definitely be dated prior to the Padua frescoes (1511) because its poetic mood is characteristic of Titian's style when he was still under Giorgione's influence.

Fig. 6
PORTRAIT OF A YOUNG MAN. Canvas, 39¹/₄ x 33 in. (100 x 84 cm.) London, Earl of Halifax Collection.

Listed in the inventory of the Ingram collection at Temple Newsman in 1808 and mentioned by Waagen (1854, II, 334) as a portrait of Martin Bucer by Titian, the painting was attributed to Giorgione by Cook.

Generally recognized as an authentic work by Titian of the period around 1515, but probably painted a few years earlier.

Fig. 7

MAN IN A RED CAP. Canvas, 31 x 26³/₄ in. (79 x 68 cm.) New York, Frick Collection.

Formerly in the Lane Collection, Dublin.

Attributed to Titian by Berenson (1932), accepted by most scholars as authentic, but omitted in Tietze's list of the master's originals and ascribed to Giorgione by Coletti (1955).

Assigned by Morassi (1954) to the period prior to the Padua frescoes but later than 1515 by Pallucchini (1954).

Fig. 8

PORTRAIT OF A MAN WEARING A PLUMED HAT. Canvas, 31³/₄ x 25 in. (81 x 63.5 cm.) Egremont, National Trust, Petworth House.

Formerly in the Earl of Leconfield collection and probably to be identified with the painting mentioned by Waagen (1854, III, 34) as a work by Titian. The painting was listed, however, as belonging to the Northern school, 16th century, in the *Petworth catalogue* (1920, 62) compiled by Collins Baker.

Published by Morassi (1956) as authentic and tentatively identified as the *Portrait of Giorgione* executed by his young pupil Titian prior to the Padua murals about 1510. The attribution to Titian has been accepted by Berenson and Pallucchini.

Fig. 9

ASSUMPTION OF THE VIRGIN. Panel, 239³/₄ x 141³/₄ in. (609 x 360 cm.) Venice, S. Maria dei Frari.

Signed and dated: TICIANUS MDXVI.

Commissioned early in 1516 by Father Germano of the Franciscan Monastery of S. Maria dei Frari, and installed on the altar in the main apse of the church on March 20, 1518 (M. Sanudo, Diary, 1496-1513), on the feast day of Saint Bernardino, when the Venetians used to flock to the church to hear the sermons of the Franciscan monks. (Ridolfi reported (1648) that Titian worked on the panel at the monastery itself where he was annoyed by the Father Superior's frequent visits and by his objections to the excessive size of the Apostles. Titian, however, intended them to be in proportion with the vast and solemn space for which the painting was destined.) When the work was finished, there were rumors, confirmed by Dolce (1557, 56, " . . . the daubers and the rabble . . . made every effort to disparage the panel "), that, in view of the friars' apparent dissatisfaction, Titian wanted to take the painting back, but desisted from doing so only when Father Germano hastened to praise it in public, prompted no doubt by the persistent efforts of the emperor's envoy, Adorno, who made tempting financial offers to obtain the altarpiece for his sovereign.

In 1568 Vasari said the *Assumption* was already " in poor condition" and "barely discernible." Reynolds found it to be " very dark " in 1752. Repeatedly restored, the painting was removed in 1818 and kept at the Academy until 1919 when it was returned to its original place.

Fig. 10

Polyptych. RESURRECTION OF CHRIST. Panel. Center panel, 101¹/₂ x 48 in. (278 x 122 cm.) Each lower lateral panel, 67 x 25¹/₂ in. (170 x 65 cm.) Each upper lateral panel, 31 x 25¹/₂ in. (79 x 65 cm.) Brescia, Church of SS. Nazzaro and Celso.

Signed and dated: TICIANUS FACIEBAT / MDXXII on the fallen column seen on the ground in the *Saint Sebastian*.

The polyptych, commissioned by the papal legate in Venice, Altobello Alveroldi, consists of five parts showing the *Resurrection* in the center; *Saints Nazzaro and Celso with Kneeling Donor* and *Saint Sebastian* in the lower side panels; the *Angel of the Annunciation* and the *Virgin* in the upper side panels.

The *Saint Sebastian* was already completed in 1522 when, through Giacomo Tebaldi, ambassador of the court of the Estes in Venice, it was offered to the Duke of Ferrara as compensation for Titian's slowness in finishing the Bacchanalian scenes. The offer was rejected by Alfonso d'Este who feared he might make an enemy of Averoldi.

There were apparently several copies of the *Saint Sebastian*, one of which, sent to Mantua in 1530, later found its way into the collection of Charles I of England. Drawings for the *Saint Sebastian* are now at the Staedel Institut in Frankfurt and at the Kupferstichkabinett in Berlin. (See Figs. 30, 31.)

Fig. 11

THE MADONNA OF THE PESARO FAMILY. Canvas, 188¹/₄ x 105¹/₂ in. (478 x 268 cm.) Venice, S. Maria dei Frari.

Executed by Titian for Jacopo Pesaro, Bishop of Paphus, in charge of the papal galleries. The altarpiece was commissioned on April 24, 1519, for the Altar of the Conception in the Church of the Frari but installed on December 8, 1526. The Pesaro archives contain receipts of payment dating from April 1519 to May 1526.

The large votive painting shows the Bishop Jacopo Pesaro and other members of the Pesaro family in prayer before the Madonna enthroned with the Child and Saints. The banner on the left displays the coat of arms of the Borgia and Pesaro families. The figure of the Turk symbolizes the Pesaros' victory over the infidels with the Venetian and papal fleets at Santa Maura in 1502.

There exists a previous votive picture with the Bishop Pesaro and Pope Alexander VI (Borgia) before Saint Peter (Antwerp Museum), which shows the naval encounter at Santa Maura in the background. (See also Plate 14.)

Fig. 12

BACCHUS AND ARIADNE. Canvas, 68³/₄ x 74³/₄ in. (175 x 190 cm.) London, National Gallery.

Signed TICIANUS F.

Cited by Lomazzo (1548) in Ferrara and taken to Rome by Cardinal Aldobrandini in 1598 when the dukedom of Ferrara was incorporated into the papal state. After having shared in the destiny of the Aldobrandini family throughout the centuries, the painting was sold to an Englishman named A. Day in 1803 and came to the National Gallery in 1826 from the Hamlet Collection.

The work is one of the three Bacchanalian scenes painted by Titian for the Alabaster Chamber of the Duke of Ferrara. The correspondence of the Duke's envoy in Venice, Giacomo Tebaldi, with Alfonso d'Este disclosed that the work, based on texts of Ovid, Nonnus and Catullus, was in the process of execution in 1522 and finished at the beginning of 1523. (See Campori, 1874 and Gronau, 1928.) The entire series of paintings commissioned for the decoration of Alfonso d'Este's chambers are believed to have included also the famous *Feast of the Gods* by Giovanni Bellini (National Gallery, Washington) and the *Triumph of Cybele* by Dossi (London). (See E. Battisti, *Commentari*, 1954.)

Fig. 13

PORTRAIT OF FRANCESCO ACQUAVIVA, DUKE OF ATRI. (?). Canvas, 87³/₄ x 59¹/₂ in. (223 x 151 cm.) Kassel Gallery.

Once tentatively identified as the portrait of the Marquis del Vasto, Alfonso d'Avalos, and subsequently as that of Giovanni Francisco Acquaviva, Duke of Atri (Justi, 1894). Allegedly painted by Titian in 1552, the year in which Aretino praised the painting in a letter to the Duke written in August. However, comparison with an authentic portrait of the Duke (Hadeln, 1934) has made this identification doubtful for reasons of obvious dissimilarities of facial characteristics.

The date ca. 1549-50, suggested by Cavalcaselle (II, 439), has now been generally accepted. The dog in the painting appears with a child and a fire in the background in a canvas at the Museum in Rotterdam.

Fig. 14

PORTRAIT OF DON DIEGO MENDOZA. Canvas, 69¹/₄ x 44 in. (176 x 112 cm.) Florence, Pitti Palace.

Vasari reported that Titian painted the portrait in 1541 of Don Diego Mendoza, ambassador of Charles V to Venice, and commended the artist for showing the illustrious Mendoza in full length. That the canvas now in the Pitti Palace is Mendoza's portrait has been questioned some scholars, as, for instance, by Gronau (1904) who dated the work ca. 1548, and by Tietze (1950) who proposed a date ca. 1545-50. I am inclined to agree with the suggested identity, especially since stylistically the date of 1541 appears most probable for the work in question.

Fig. 15

VENUS OF PARDO. Canvas, 77 x 151¹/₂ in. (196 x 385 cm.) Paris, Louvre.

The picture has sometimes been identified with the *Nude in a Landscape with a Satyr* which Titian, in a letter dated December 22, 1574 (Archives Simancas, Leg. 1396) says he sent to Philip II in 1567. Some scholars believe it is the *Sleeping Venus with Satyrs* mentioned by Lomazzo (1590) as belonging to the painter's son Pomponio who had inherited it from his father. (For further details, see the notes to Plate 28.)

Fig. 16

PORTRAIT OF CLARICE STROZZI. Canvas, 45¹/₄ x 38¹/₂ in. (115 x 98 cm.) Berlin, Staatliche Museum.

Signed and dated: TITIANUS F. ANNOR. II MDXLII.

This portrait of the little daughter of Roberto Strozzi, a famous patron of art and literature, was praised highly by Aretino in a letter to Titian written in July, 1542. The painting was acquired from the Palazzo Strozzi in 1878.

Fig. 17

CHARLES V ON HORSEBACK. Canvas, 130³/₄ x 109³/₄ in. (332 x 279 cm.) Madrid, Prado.

Listed in the catalogue of paintings owned by Mary of Hungary, the sister of Charles V, this work was taken to Spain where it was known to be at the Casa del Tesoro in 1600 and later in the Pardo Palace, where it was damaged in a fire in 1608. The Emperor is shown departing for the victorious battle of Mühlberg fought against the Protestants on the banks of the Elbe river on April 24, 1547.

Titian painted the portrait between April and September, 1548, in Augsburg while the imperial Diet was in session. Restored shortly afterwards by C. Amberger (see Beinert, 1946).

Fig. 18

VOTIVE PORTRAIT OF THE VENDRAMIN FAMILY. Canvas, 81 x 118¹/₂ in. (206 x 301 cm.) London, National Gallery.

A work definitely identical with the one described in the catalogue of the Gabriele Vendramin collection in March, 1569: " a large picture . . . with Sir Andrea Vendramin, his seven sons and Sir Gabriel Vendramin . . . by the hand of Sir Titian." The painting probably remained in Venice until 1636, then became part of van Dyck's collection. It was purchased by the Dukes of Northumberland ca. 1645-46 and finally by the National Gallery in 1929. For further details see the notes to Plate 26.

Fig. 19

PIETRO ARETINO. Canvas, 38¹/₂ x 30³/₄ in. (98 x 78 cm.) Florence, Pitti Palace.

This work has been generally recognized as the portrait repeatedly mentioned by Aretino in his letters of

1545 to Giovio and Cosimo de Medici, and described in one of them as a " stupendous wonder." Immediately upon delivery of the painting, Aretino sent it to the Grand Duke in Florence, informing Cosimo of the shipment on October 17, 1545 (Gaye, II, 331), and insinuating that " if more money had been spent... the clothes might have been bright, stiff and rigid like true satin, velvet and brocade... " Aretino also complained to Titian in a letter to Rome that his portrait appeared to him to be a sketch rather than a finished painting. He continued to bombard the Grand Duke with letters of reproach for not thanking him for the gift until he finally received an amount of money. (See Gaye, op. cit.)

Fig. 20

VENUS AND ADONIS. Canvas, 73^1/$_4$ x 81^1/$_2$ in. (186 x 207 cm.) Madrid, Prado.

In a letter to Giovanni Benevides dated September 10, 1554, Titian referred to the shipment to Philip of Spain of a " poetical " work showing *Venus and Adonis* (Ticozzi, 1817, 312). He meant the picture now in the Prado which reached the Prince in London where he had gone to be married to Mary Tudor. Philip complained to Vargas in December, 1554, that the painting had arrived in poor condition. The picture was known to have been at the Alcazar in 1636, at the Casa de Rebeque in 1794, and at the Academy of Madrid from 1796 to 1827.

Other versions are in the National Gallery, London, the National Gallery, Washington, the Metropolitan Museum, New York, and the National Gallery, Rome. The latter was executed in part by assistants.

Fig. 21

DIANA AND ACTAEON. Canvas, 70^1/$_4$ x 78 in. (179 x 198 cm.) London, Earl of Harewood Collection (now in the National Gallery).

The painting is one of the " poetic " subjects painted by Titian for Philip II (*Diana and Actaeon;* and *Diana and Callisto*, Edinburgh; *The Rape of Europa*, Boston; *Venus and Adonis*, Prado; etc.). In a letter dated June 19, 1559, Titian informed the King that he had begun painting this picture.

The painting probably passed from the Spanish royal collections to those of the Archduke Leopold William (where it was copied by Tenier and published in *Teatrum Pictorium* as an engraving in 1660). Subsequent owners were Christina of Sweden, 1689; Azzolini Collection; Odescalchi Collection; Lord Alford; Earl of Brownlow; and Lord Harewood, 1919.

Fig. 22

THE RAPE OF EUROPA. Canvas, 70 x 80^3/$_4$ in. (178 x 205 cm.) Boston, Isabella Stewart Gardner Museum.

Signed: TITIANUS F.

This, one of the " poetic subjects " painted for Philip

II, was mentioned by Titian as being in the process of execution in a letter to the King, June 19, 1559. Further references to the picture were made in letters of April 22, 1560, April 2, 1561, August 17, 1561 and, finally, April 26, 1562 when Titian informed Philip of the shipment of the finished painting. Cited at the beginning of the 18th century in the collection of the Duke of Grammont and next in that of the Duke of Orleans, the painting was sold in London on May 7, 1804 to Lord Berwick. Later it passed into the collection of Lord Darnley at Cobham Hall. Finally, the picture was acquired by Berenson in 1896 for the Gardner Museum in Boston.

The painting was copied by Rubens and van Dyck.

Fig. 23

DESCENT OF THE HOLY SPIRIT. Canvas, 185 x 102^1/$_4$ in. (570 x 260 cm.) Venice, Santa Maria della Salute.

According to Vasari (1568), " In 1541, Titian painted an altarpiece for the friars of Santo Spirito in Venice depicting the descent of the Holy Spirit to the Apostles, God being shown in the form of fire, the Spirit as a dove. Because the painting deteriorated slightly, there was much litigation with those friars, and a copy had to be made which is the one now on the altar."

It was the new version, repainted to replace the disfigured one and so significant for the understanding of the formative stage of El Greco's art, which was seen by Vasari in its original site. The work may be dated ca. 1555 (as suggested by Fogolari, 1935) or 1560 (the date proposed by Tietze).

Fig. 24

THE MARTYRDOM OF SAINT LAWRENCE. Canvas, 196^3/$_4$ x 109^1/$_2$ in. (500 x 278 cm.) Venice, Santa Maria dei Gesuiti.

The signature TITIANUS VECELLIUS AEQUES F. was found to be counterfeit when the painting was restored in 1959 (Valcanover, 1960, II, p. 40).

Commissioned by Lorenzo Massolo for the decoration of his tomb in the church of the Crociferi (later of the Jesuits) and conceived as a fantastic " nocturne," the painting was in the process of work in November, 1548, as indicated in Massolo's last will. It must have been installed between 1557, the year of the client's death, and 1559 when it was already known to be in the church of the Crociferi. A slightly different version was painted later by Titian for Philip II of Spain who was notified by the painter on December 2, 1567, of the forthcoming shipment of the picture. It is now in the Monastery of Saint Lawrence at the Escorial.

Fig. 25

SAINT SEBASTIAN. Canvas, 83^1/$_2$ x 45^1/$_2$ in. (212 x 116 cm.) Leningrad, Hermitage.

At Titian's death (1576) the painting was still in his studio. It went to his son Pomponio, who sold it in 1581 to Cristoforo Barbarigo, a patrician of Venice, from whose descendents it was purchased together with the *Magdalene* for the Leningrad gallery in 1850.

The painting, generally dated after 1570, is one of the most moving masterpieces of Titian's last years.

In Cavalcaselle's times (II, 492) the poor condition of the picture prevented its exhibition at the museum.

Fig. 26

THE FLAYING OF MARSYAS. Canvas, 83 1/2 x 81 1/2 in. (212 x 207 cm.) Kromieriz, Czechoslovakia, Gallery.

Attributed to Titian in an auction sale in Vienna in 1670, the painting was bought by the Bishop of Olmütz in 1673. Ignored in the Titian literature until 1909 when it was mentioned by Frimmel, the work was subsequently published by Benesch in 1928. It is one of Titian's masterpieces painted in the style of his old age.

Fig. 27

MADONNA WITH SAINTS AND THE ARTIST. Canvas, 39 1/4 x 55 in (100 x 140 cm.) Pieve di Cadore, Archbishop's Church.

" In Cadore, his home country, Titian painted a picture with Our Lady, the Bishop Saint Titian and the artist himself kneeling. " (Vasari, 1568.) This quotation from Vasari definitely refers to the small votive painting at Pieve di Cadore. Here, according to a tradition going back to Anonimo del Tizianello (1622), we recognize Francesco Vecellio, Titian's elder brother who died in 1559, in the image of Saint Andrew; Marco Vecellio, the master's nephew and pupil, in the head of Saint Titian; and the artist himself easily recognizable as the man in black holding a crosier.

Titian and some of his closest assistants went to Pieve di Cadore in 1565 to look into the matter of the frescoes for the apse of the Archbishop's church which were painted later by his pupils. Either then or shortly afterwards he painted the altarpiece for the family chapel, but in any event, not later than in the year it was recorded by Vasari.

Fig. 28

THE JEALOUS HUSBAND. Pen Drawing, 7 3/8 x 7 in. (188 x 177 mm.) Paris, Ecole des Beaux-Arts.

This is a preparatory drawing for one of the three murals in the Scuola del Santo in Padua painted by Titian in 1511. We have here an early work of Titian's graphic art showing a power and ardor unparalleled in Venetian art at that time. Influenced by Dürer in certain respects.

Fig. 29

PORTRAIT OF A WOMAN. Chalk drawing on hazel paper, 16 1/2 x 10 3/8 in. (419 x 265 mm.) Florence, Uffizi.

From the outset, Titian's drawing style seems free and unhampered by the tradition of Bellini, and after some concessions to Dürer's forms, he moved closer to Giorgione's art, acquiring a style that is more atmospheric, softer in tonality, and more monumental than Giorgione's. This drawing, once attributed to Giorgione, resembles in its broad modeling the so-called *Portrait of a Slavonian Lady* in the National Gallery, London, and the figure of the young mother in the mural with *Saint Anthony Granting Speech to an Infant* in the Scuola del Santo at Padua (Plates 2, 3).

Fig. 30

STUDIES FOR THE SAINT SEBASTIAN IN BRESCIA. Pen Drawing on white paper, 6 3/8 x 5 3/8 in. (162 x 136 mm.) Berlin, Kupferstichkabinett.

A preparatory sketch for the figure of Saint Sebastian completed in 1522 for the Averoldi polyptych in the church of Saints Nazzaro and Celso in Brescia (see Fig. 10). The softness of Titian's early drawings have given way here to forcefulness and exceptional impetuosity.

Tietze (1944) suggested that the figure of the Madonna with the Child on this drawing may have been an early idea for the altarpiece now at the Museo Civico of Ancona and dated 1520.

Fig. 31

STUDY FOR THE SAINT SEBASTIAN IN BRESCIA. Pen drawing, 7 1/4 x 4 1/2 in. (183 x 114 mm.) Frankfurt, Städelsches Institut.

Preparatory drawing for the figure of Saint Sebastian completed in 1522 for the Averoldi altarpiece in Brescia. The Saint is conceived in a more definite and precise stance, rendered with surprising plasticity in strokes that are sharp and ordered.

On the reverse: studies of a head in profile, feet, and parts of a leg.

Fig. 32

JUPITER AND IO. Charcoal drawing on bluish paper, 8 7/8 x 10 3/8 in. (225 x 265 mm.) Cambridge, Fitzwilliam Museum, Charles Ricketts Collection.

A drawing from Titian's late period, done in an expressionist style which tends to grasp the essence rather than the whole form by means of a new rhythm of agitated and explosive lines.

A copy of this drawing is in the Louvre.

BIOGRAPHICAL SKETCH

1488 - 1490 Probable date of Titian's birth at Pieve di Cadore.

1508 - Titian, with his teacher Giorgione, painted the murals of the Fondaco dei Tedeschi (Dolce, Vasari). The building had been destroyed by fire in 1505 and completely rebuilt between May 1507 and May 1508.

1510 - Giorgione died of the plague in Venice.

1511 - Titian painted the frescoes of the three miracles of Saint Anthony at the Scuola del Santo in Padua, begun on April 23, and received the balance of four gold ducats on December 2.

1513 - Titian declined Pietro Bembo's invitation to the papal court in Rome and promised to paint a battle-scene for the Hall of the Great Council in the Ducal Palace in return for the broker's patent of the Fondaco dei Tedeschi. In the same year he established his workshop at San Samuele. His assistants were Antonio Buxei and Ludovico di Giovanni.

1516 - Father Germano of the Frari Monastery commissioned Titian to paint the altarpiece of the *Assumption.*
Titian established contact with the court of Ferrara which he visited from January 31 to March 22. Giovanni Bellini died, one of Titian's first teachers, according to tradition.

1517 - Titian painted a bathing scene for the Duke of Ferrara.

1518 - The altarpiece of the *Assumption* was unveiled at the Church of the Frari on Saint Bernardino's Day, March 20 (Sanudo, Diary). Titian worked on the first of the Bacchanalian scenes for Alfonso d'Este (see the correspondence of the Duke and his representative in Venice, Giacomo Tebaldi).

1519 - Jacopo Pesaro commissioned Titian to do an altarpiece for the Altar of the Conception in the Church of the Frari on April 24. Titian arrived in Ferrara with the first of the Bacchanalian scenes.

1520 - Titian placed the date on the altar painting for the church of San Francesco in Ancona, commissioned by Alvise Gozzi.
In reply to urgent requests for the remaining two Bacchanalian scenes, the painter offered the Duke of Ferrara the *Saint Sebastian* of the polyptych commissioned by Averoldi. The Duke refused.

1521 - Titian arrived in Brescia.

1522 - Titian signed and dated the polyptych for the church of Saint Nazzaro and Saint Celso, commissioned by the papal legate Altobello Averoldi.
The artist worked on *Bacchus and Ariadne* for Alfonso d'Este (according to Tebaldi's letters).

1523 - Journey to Ferrara.
Titian painted an unidentified portrait for the Marquis of Mantua.
According to tradition the newly elected Doge Andrea Gritti commissioned Titian to paint the *Saint Christopher* at the Ducal Palace.

1524 - Titian revisited Ferrara in November. Giulio Romano arrived in Mantua.

1525 - Titian married Cecilia.
(The Doge Gritti conferred titles on Titian's relatives.)

1526 - Installation of the *Pesaro Altarpiece,* commissioned in 1519, at the Church of the Frari.

1527 - Pietro Aretino established residence in Venice. Fleeing from the sack of Rome, Sansovino and Sebastiano del Piombo arrived in Venice. The painter became a friend of Aretino and Sansovino.

1528 - Titian is once again in Ferrara, in a competition held by the Brotherhood of Saint Peter Martyr for a painting for the high altar of the church of San Giovanni e San Paolo. Titian won over Palma Vecchio and Pordenone.

1529 - Titian spent some time in Mantua.

Michelangelo arrived in Venice in the autumn.
Clemens VII and Charles V met in Bologna.

1530 - Titian went to Bologna to paint the portrait of Emperor Charles V.
On April 27 the altarpiece of *Saint Peter Martyr* was unveiled at the church of San Giovanni e Paolo.
The artist's wife, Cecilia, died on August 5.

1531 - Gonzaga (for whom Titian designed silverware) granted the artist's son, Pomponio Vecellio, the parish of Medole. Sanudo saw the votive painting, later destroyed, of the Doge Gritti exhibited at the Ducal Palace.
Titian moved his studio to the San Canciano (region) at Birri Grande.

1532 - Giacomo Leonardi, ambassador of the Duke of Urbino in Venice, reported that Titian was working on a figure of *Christ,* a *Nativity* and a *Portrait of Hannibal* for della Rovere.

1533 - Titian traveled to Bologna where he painted the portrait of Charles V. In return, honorary titles were awarded to him and his sons.

1534 - The *Nativity* painted for the Duke of Urbino was received in Pesaro.
Titian painted a *Portrait of Isabella d'Este* representing her as a young woman.

1535 - The paintings of *Christ* and the *Portrait of Hannibal* were received in Pesaro.

1536 - Titian painted the *Portrait of Francesco Maria della Rovere* clad in armor, and the *Duchess Eleonora of Urbino* (Uffizi).
Federico Gonzaga expressed the desire to have a hall of his palace in Mantua decorated with portraits of the twelve Roman Emperors now lost, which Titian was commissioned to do.

1537 - Four of the twelve paintings of *Emperors* were in place. Titian sent Isabella of Spain an *Annunciation* originally painted for the nuns of Santa Maria degli Angeli at Murano.

1538 - Titian lost his right to the broker's patent of the Fondaco dei Tedeschi because of his failure to complete the *Battle* promised in 1513.

1539 - The broker's patent of the Fondaco dei Tedeschi was restored to Titian.
He painted portraits of the newly elected Doge Pietro Lando; Charles V; Francis I of France; and the Turk Suleiman for Guidobaldo II della Rovere, successor to Francesco Maria della Rovere who had died in 1538.

1540 - Titian painted portraits of Alessandro degli Organi, Pietro Bembo, and Vincenzo Cappello.

1541 - The *Allocution* commissioned by Alfonso d'Avalos (Prado) was received in Milan.
Titian painted the portrait of *Don Diego Mendoza.*
Vasari stayed in Venice from December to the beginning of 1542.

1542 - Titian completed the portraits of *Clarice Strozzi* and *Ranuccio Farnese;* a votive painting for the Doge Pietro Lando; and a *Nativity* for the cathedral of Novara.

1543 - Charles V and Pope Paul III met at Ferrara. Titian painted the Pope's portrait.

1545 - Titian painted portraits of Daniele Barbaro; Guidobaldo II; and one of Aretino which was sent to Cosimo de' Medici.
Titian left for Rome in autumn in response to a new invitation from the Farnese family. He passed through Pesaro and Urbino in September and, provided with an escort by the Duke, arrived in Rome in October, where he was given a princely welcome by Pope Paul III, Bembo, and Cardinal Farnese. He met Vasari. Sebastiano del Piombo, and Michelangelo, and painted various portraits for the Farnese (Capo di Monte Gallery, Naples), also a *Magdalene,* an *Ecce Homo,* and the famous *Danae.*

1546 - Honorary Roman citizenship was awarded Titian for his " merits and services. "
On his return to Venice he stopped off in Florence where he offered his services to Cosimo de' Medici who refused to accept them.
Titian painted the portrait of the Doge Francesco Donato.

1547 - Unveiling of the altarpiece at the Cathedral of Serravalle, a painting on which the artist had worked since 1542 and which gave rise to litigations lasting until 1553.
Following Sebastiano del Piombo's death, Titian applied for the now vacant office of " Keeper of the Seal " which, however, was conferred on Gerolamo della Porta.
Charles V summoned the painter to Augsburg.

1548 - Titian left for Augsburg in January accompanied by his son Orazio, his nephew Cesare Vecelli, and his pupil Lambert Sustris. He took with him an *Ecce Homo* to be given to the Emperor. During his stay in Augsburg the artist portrayed Charles V and all the important members who had convened for the Diet. Returning to Venice, Titian stopped at Innsbruck for more portrait painting and arrived in Venice in October. In December he went to Milan and painted the portrait of Philip, the son of Charles V.

1549 - Titian painted portraits of Philip for the Chancellor Granvelle and of Charles V for Ferrante Gonzaga. Engravings were made by Domenico delle Greche of Titian's painting *Overthrow of Pharoah in the Red Sea.*

1550 - Titian arrived in Augsburg in November and again painted Philip's portrait.

1551 - Titian returned to Venice.

1552 - Titian began his correspondence with Prince Philip, informing him of the shipment of a *Landscape* and a *Saint Margaret.* On October 29, the Venetian authorities awarded him the broker's patent for the salt-trade.

1553 - The artist worked on a number of " poetic subjects " for Philip of Spain. He also painted portraits of the Bishop Beccadelli and the new Doge Marcantonio Trevisan.

1554 - To Charles V in Flanders Titian sent the *Holy Trinity,* which accompanied the Emperor into his voluntary retirement at San Juste, and a *Mater Dolorosa.* To Philip in England he shipped the " poetic subject " *Venus and Adonis* that autumn. To the church of Santa Maria di Medole he donated an altarpiece representing the Resurrection in order to obtain the office of canon for one of his nephews which had been taken away from his son Pomponio.

1555 - Marriage of the artist's daughter Lavinia to Cornelio Sarcinelli of Serravalle.
Titian finished the portrait of the Doge Francesco Venier elected the year before. This completed the series of doge portraits executed by Titian who continued to keep the broker's patent.

1556 - On January 28, the artist received the balance of his fee for the votive painting of the Doge Trevisan, which was installed above the door of the Sala dei Pregadi and destroyed in 1575.
Death of Pietro Aretino.
Titian was invited to join the jury of the competition for the decoration of the ceilings in the library designed by Sansovino.

1557 - After reconciliation with his son Pomponio, the artist obtained the parish of San Andrea del Fabbio for him.
His son Orazio went to Milan to collect a pension owed him.
In November a *Deposition* destined for Philip II was lost by the postmaster of Trento.

1558 - Death of Charles V.
Philip II ordered the governor of Milan to pay Titian his overdue pension.

1559 - Death of Francesco Vecellio, the artist's brother.
The painter informed Philip II that he had sent him the " poetic paintings, " *Diana and Actaeon*

and *Diana and Callisto* and a *Deposition,* and that he was working on two more " poetic subjects, " *The Rape of Europa* and *The Death of Actaeon* as well as a religious work, *Christ in the Garden.*
The Martyrdom of Saint Lawrence, commissioned by Lorenzo Massolo in November, 1548, is placed in the church of the Crociferi.

1560 - Letters were sent to Philip II regarding the progress being made on the *Rape of Europa* and *Christ in the Garden.*

1562 - The *Rape of Europa* and *Christ in the Garden* were shipped to Spain.

1563 - Progress reports were made to Philip II on *The Lord's Supper* commissioned in 1558.

1564 - *The Lord's Supper* was finished and sent to Philip II.
In October Titian traveled to Brescia for the contract of three canvases for the ceiling of the hall in the Palazzo Pubblico.

1565 - Titian went to Pieve di Cadore with Cesare Vecellio, Emanuele of Augsburg, and Valerio Zuccato to discuss the frescoes for the local church which were executed later by his pupils.

1566 - Titian obtained from the Council of Ten exclusive royalty rights on a number of engravings made by Cornelio Cort and Nicolo Boldrini after his pictures. In May, Vasari visited Titian at his home in Birri (Venice) where he took notes of the paintings he saw in the artist's studio.
With Andrea Palladio and Tintoretto, Titian was elected a member of the Academy of Tuscan Painters.

1567 - Titian gave the Duke of Urbino a *Madonna.* To Pius V and to Cardinal Farnese he presented a *Magdalene,* a *Saint Peter Martyr,* and a *Saint Catherine.*
In a letter of December 2, to Philip II, the artist reported the completion of the *Martyrdom of Saint Lawrence.*

1568 - Installation of the three canvases commissioned in 1564 for the Palazzo Pubblico, Brescia. They had been completed in 1567, and have since been destroyed.
Titian informed Philip II of the completion of *The Tribute Money,* now in the National Gallery, London.
He asked the antiquarian Jacopo Strada to offer Emperor Maximilian II a number of paintings, now lost, of poetic subjects identical to those executed for Philip II: *Diana and Endymion, Diana and Actaeon, Diana and Callisto, Death of Actaeon, Venus and Adonis, Perseus and Andromeda,* and *The Rape of Europa.*

1569 - Titian's request that the broker's patent for the salt trade be transferred to his son Orazio was granted.

1570 - Sansovino, for many years a close friend of Titian's, died on November 27.

1571 - Titian sent Philip II the *Roman Lucretia* and had his pension in Milan transferred to his son Orazio.

1572 - With the permission of Venetian authorities, the French ambassador selected some paintings at the painter's studio.

1574 - On a trip to Venice, Henry III of France visited the studio of the aging painter.
In a letter of December 22, to Antonio Perez, the King's secretary, asking for payment, Titian listed many of the paintings sent to Philip II in the course of the years.

1575 - Titian sent Philip II a further request for payment for his numerous works and in September shipped to Spain the *Allegory of the Battle of Lepanto* and *Religion Defended by Spain.*

1576 - On February 27, Titian addressed his last letter to Philip II requesting payment for his pictures.
Titian died of the plague on August 27, and was buried at the Church of the Frari on August 28. His son Orazio died only a few days later, and the artist's large house at the Birri, so rich in art treasures and memories but now unguarded, was pillaged.

BIBLIOGRAPHY OF MAJOR PUBLICATIONS

1496 - 1533 M. Sanudo, *I diarii*, Venice.

1521 - 1543 M. Michiel, *Notizie d'opere di disegno* (Ms. Biblioteca Marciana, ed. J. Morelli, Bassano 1880; ed. G. Frizzoni, Bologna 1884; ed. T. Frimmel, Vienna 1887).

1537 - 1557 P. Aretino, *Lettere*, 6 vol. Venice.

1548 - P. Pino, *Dialogo di pittura*, Venice.

1557 - L. Dolce, *Dialogo della pittura*, Venice.

1568 - G. Vasari, *Le Vite* (I ed. 1550), Florence.

1581 - F. Sansovino, *Venetia città nobilissima*, Venice.

1584 - G. P. Lomazzo, *Trattato dell'arte della pittura*, Milan.

1622 - Tizianello, *Breve Compendio della vita del famoso Tiziano Vecellio di Cadore*, Venice.

1648 - C. Ridolfi, *Le meraviglie dell'arte*, Venice.

1660 - M. Boschini, *La carta del navegar pittoresco*, Venice.

1674 - M. Boschini, *Le ricche miniere*, Venice.

1681 - F. Baldinucci, *Notizie dei Professori del disegno*, Florence.

1683 - J. De Sandrart, *Accademia nobilissimae artis pictoriae*, Nuremberg.

1704 - P. Orlandi, *Abecedario Pittorico*, Bologna.

1715 - G. B. Milesio, *Descrizione del Fondaco dei Tedeschi* (ed. M. Brunetti, *Il Fondaco nostro dei Tedeschi*, Venice 1941).

1739 - 1740 C. De Brosses, *Lettres d'Italie* (ed. Paris 1858).

1740 - A. M. Zanetti, *Varie pitture a fresco de' principali maestri veneziani*, Venice.

1762 - F. Algarotti, *Saggio sopra la pittura*, Venice.

1771 - A. M. Zanetti, *Della pittura veneziana*, Venice (II ed. 1792).

1789 - L. Lanzi, *Storia pittorica d'Italia*, Bassano.

1817 - S. Ticozzi, *Vite dei pittori Vecelli di Cadore*, Milan.

1840 - G. Gaye, *Carteggio inedito d'artisti*, Florence.

1854 - T. Gar - B. Malfatti, *Lettera di G. della Torre a Cristoforo Madruzzo del 1548*, in « Calendario Trentino per l'anno 1854 ».

1854 - D. Gonzati, *La Basilica del Santo*, Padua.

1854 - 1857 G. F. Waagen, *Treasures of Art in Great Britain*, London.

1855 - J. Burckhardt, *Der Cicerone*, Basel.

1864 - A. Ronchini, *Delle relazioni di Tiziano coi Farnese*, in « Atti e Memorie delle RR. Dep. di storia patria per le prov. modenesi e parmensi ».

1866 - G. Campori, *Lettere artistiche inedite*, Modena.

1874 - G. Campori, *Tiziano e gli Estensi*, in « Nuova Antologia ».

1877 - 1878 J. A. Crowe - G. B. Cavalcaselle, *Tiziano, la sua vita e i suoi tempi*, Florence, 2 vol.

1879 - G. Cadorin, *Dei tre quadroni dipinti da Tiziano per la sala del Pubblico Palazzo di Brescia*, Venice.

1880 - G. Morelli (J. Lermolieff), *Die Werke italienischer Meister in den Galerien von München, Dresden und Berlin*, Leipzig.

1881 - W. Braghirolli, *Tiziano alla corte dei Gonzaga di Mantova*, in « Atti e Memorie della R. Accademia virgiliana di Mantova ».

1886 - G. Lafenestre, *La vie et l'œuvre du Titien*, Paris.

1890 - G. Morelli, *Kunstkritische Studien über italienische Malerei. Die Galerie Borghese u. Doria*, Leipzig, (it. ed., Milan 1897).

1893 - G. Morelli, *Die Galerie zu Berlin*, Leipzig.

1893 - A. Venturi, *Il Museo e la Galleria Borghese*, Rome.

1893 - F. Wickhoff, *Les écoles italiennes au Musée impérial de Vienne*, in « Gazette des Beaux-Arts ».

1894 - B. Berenson, *The Venetian Painters of the Renaissance*, New York and London.

1894 - C. Justi, *Tizian und Alfonso von Este*, in « Jahrbuch der preuss. Kunstsammlungen ».

1894 - C. Justi, *Das Tizianbildnis der Kön. Gal. zu Kassel*, in «Jahrbuch der preuss. Kunstsammlungen».

1897 - C. Justi, *Die Bildnisse des Kardinals Hyppolit von Medici in Florenz*, in « Zeitschrift für bildende Kunst ».

1897 - C. Phillips, *The earlier Work of Titian*, London.

1898 - H. Knackfuss, *Tizian*, Bielefeld, Leipzig.

1898 - C. Phillips, *Titian: a study of his life and works*, London.

1900 - G. Gronau, *Tizian*, Berlin (Eng. ed. London 1904).

1902 - F. Wickhoff, *Die « Andrier des Philostrat » von Tizian*, in « Jahrbuch der preuss. Kunstsammlungen ».

1903 - M. Hamel, *Titien*, Paris.

1904 - O. Fischel, *Tizian.* (Klassiker der Kunst), Stuttgart (II ed. 1906, III ed. 1907, V ed. 1924).

1904 - 1906 G. Gronau, *Die Kunstbestrebungen der Herzöge von Urbino*, in « Jahrbuch der preuss. Kunstsammlungen » 1904 - 1906.

1904 - C. Justi, *Tizian und der Hof von Urbino*, in «Jahrbuch der preuss. Kunstsammlungen».

1906 - P. Kristeller, *Il Trionfo della Fede*, Berlin.

1908 - D. v. Hadeln, *Zu Tizian in Padua*, in « Rep. für Kunstwissenschaft ».

1908 - W. Schmidt, *Zur Kenntnis Giorgiones*, in « Rep. für Kunstwissenschaft ».

1909 - F. Frimmel, *Blätter für Gemäldekunde*, Supplement V.

1910 - C. Gerola, *Il supposto ritratto del Fracastoro dipinto dal Tiziano*, in « Archivio storico Veneto ».

1910 - C. Ricketts, *Titian*, London.

1911 - H. Ludwig, *Archivalische Beiträge zur Geschichte der venezianischen Kunst*, in « Italienische Forschungen », herausgegeben vom Kunsth. Inst. in Florenz IV. Band.

1913 - A. Luzio, *La Galleria dei Gonzaga*, Milan.

1918 - V. Basch, *Titien*, Paris.

1919 - L. Hourticq, *La jeunesse de Titien*, Paris.

1920 - T. Hetzer, *Die frühen Gemälde des Tizian*, Basel.

1920 - G. Lorenzetti, *Per la storia del «Cristo portacroce» della chiesa di San Rocco di Venezia*, in «Venezia».

1920 - A. E. Popp, *Tizians Lukrezia und Tarquinius*, in « Zeitschrift für Bild. Kunst ».

1922 - T. Borenius, *Some reflections of the last phase of Titian*, in « The Burlington Magazine ».

1922 - W. Suida, *Unbekannte Bildnisse von Tizian*, in « Belvedere ».

1922 - E. Waldmann, *Tizian*, Berlin.

1924 - D. v. Haldeln, *Zeichnungen des Tizian*, Berlin.

1925 - G. Gronau, *Concerning Titian's pictures at Alnwick Castle*, in « Apollo ».

1925 - R. Longhi, *Giunte a Tiziano*, in « L'Arte ».

1925 - A. L. Mayer, *Tizianstudien*, in « Münchner Jahrbuch d. bild. Kunst ».

1926 - G. Lorenzetti, *Venezia e il suo estuario*, Venice (II ed. 1926).

1927 - R. Longhi, *Cartella tizianesca*, in « Vita artistica ».

1927 - W. Suida, *Rivendicazioni a Tiziano*, in « Vita artistica ».

1928 - M. Dvořák, *Italienische Kunst*, Munich.

1928 - A. Foratti, *Tiziano nella Scuola del Santo*, in « Cronache d'arte ».

1928 - G. Gronau, *Alfonso d'Este und Tizian*, in « Jahrbuch der Kunstsammlungen in Wien ».

1928 - A. Venturi, *Storia dell'arte italiana, La Pittura del Cinquecento*, parte VII, vol. II, Milan 1926, part IX, vol. III. 1928.

1928 - O. Beneschi, *Die Gemäldegalerie in Kremsier*, in « Pantheon ».

1928 - 1929 C. Gamba, *La « Venere » di Giorgione reintegrata*, in « Dedalo ».

1929 - P. Beroqui, *Tiziano en el Museo del Prado*, Madrid (II ed. 1946).

1930 - G. Gronau, *Tizian*, « Klassiker der Kunst », Stuttgart.

1930 - L. Hourticq, *Le problème de Giorgione*, Paris.

1930 - H. Tietze - E. Tietze Conrat, *Tizians Studien*, in « Jahrbuch der Kunsth. Sammlungen in Wien ».

1931 - H. Posse, *Die Rekonstruktion der « Venus mit Cupido » von Giorgione*, in « Jahrbuch der preuss. Kunstsammlungen ».

1932 - B. Berenson, *Italian Pictures of the Renaissance*, Oxford.

1933 - W. Suida, *Tiziano*, Rome (German ed. Zurich, 1933; French ed. Paris, 1935).

1933 - L. Venturi, *Italian Paintings in America*, Milan.

1934 - A. Alvarez Cabanas, *La última Cena cuadro de Tiziano existente en las salas capitulares de El Escorial*, Madrid.

1934 - D. v. Hadeln, *Girolamo di Tiziano*, in « The Burlington Magazine ».

1934 - W. Suida, *New light on Titian's portraits*, in « The Burlington Magazine ».

1934 - 1936 W. Suida, *Fremde Meister um Tizian*, in « Belvedere ».

1935 - G. Fogolari, *Catalogo della Mostra di Tiziano*, Venice.

1935 - T. Hetzer, *Tizian, Geschichte seiner Farbe*, Frankfurt.

1936 - B. Berenson, *Pitture Italiane del Rinascimento*, Milan.

1936 - G. Gronau, *Documenti artistici urbinati*, Florence.

1936 - W. Suida, *Titian, die beiden Campagnola u. Ugo da Carpi*, in « Cronache d'arte ».

1936 - H. Tietze, *Tizian, Leben und Werk*, Vienna.

1936 - H. Tietze - E. Tietze Conrat, *Tizian Studien*, in « Jahrbuch der Kunsth. Sammlungen in Wien ».

1937 - G. Gronau, *Alcuni quadri di Tiziano illustrati da documenti*, in « Bollettino d'arte ».

1938 - J. Zarnoski, *L'atelier de Titien: Girolamo Dente*, in « Dawna Sztuka ».

1939 - F. Pouncey, *The Miraculous Cross in Titian's Vendramin Family*, in « Journal of the Warburg Institute » II.

1939 - A. M. Brizio, *Tiziano*, « voce » nel « Grande Dizionario Enciclopedico ». Turin, vol. X.

1940 - N. A. Gurvic, *Tiziano*, Leningrad.

1940 - T. Hetzer, *Tiziano*, in « Allgm. Künstlerlexikon » (Thieme u. Becker).

1941 - F. Mauroner, *Le incisioni di Tiziano*, Venice (II ed. 1943).

1942 - F. J. Sanchez Canton, *Catálogo del Museo del Prado*, Madrid.

1942 - A. Grappe, *Titien*, Paris.

1942 - A. Morassi, *Giorgione*, Milan.

1944 - H. Tietze - E. Tietze Conrat, *The Drawings of the Venetian Painters of the XVth and XVIth Centuries*, New York.

1944 - E. Tietze Conrat, *Titian's Battle of Cadore*, in « The Art Bulletin ».

1945 - R. Pallucchini, *Cinque secoli di pittura veneziana*, Catalogo della Mostra, Venice.

1946 - G. Fiocco, *Francesco Vecellio, Nota su Cesare Vecellio*, in « Lettere e Arti ».

1946 - B. Beinert, *Carlos V en Mühlberg, de Tiziano*, in « Archivio Español de Arte ».

1946 - R. Longhi, *Viatico per cinque secoli di pittura veneziana*, Florence.

1946 - A. Morassi, *Il Tiziano di Casa Balbi*, in « Emporium ».

1947 - B. Berenson, *Ristudiando Tintoretto e Tiziano*, in « Arte Veneta ».

1947 - G. Jedlicka, *Über einige Spätwerke von Tizian*, in « Werk ».

1947 - G. Fiocco, *Un Tiziano dimenticato*, in « Arte Veneta ».

1948 - T. Hetzer, *Tizian*, Frankfurt.

1948 - S. Ortolani, *Restauro d'un Tiziano*, in « Bollettino d'arte ».

1949 - R. Huyghe, *Le Titien*, Paris.

1950 - G. Babelon, *Titien*, Paris.

1950 - F. G. Hartlaub, *Tizian « Liebesorakel » und seine « Kristallseherin », Ein Beitrag zur weltlichen Ikonographie der Renaissance*, in « Zeitschrift für bild. Kunst ».

1950 - H. Tietze, *Titian, Paintings and Drawings*, London.

1951 - G. De Logu, *Tiziano*, Bergamo.

1951 - C. Fabbro, *Notizie storiche sul casato di Tiziano*, in « Catalogo » della Mostra di Belluno (ulteriori documenti pubbl. dallo stesso in « Archivio storico di Belluno », 1960 e 1961).

1951 - F. Valcanover, *Mostra dei Vecellio*, « Catalogo » della Mostra, Belluno.

68

1951 - E. Delacroix, *Journal*, (ed. Paris 1893). Eng. Ed. Greenwich, Conn. and London.

1951 - G. Fiocco, *I pittori Vecellio*, Dispense universitarie, Padua.

1951 - E. Tietze Conrat, *Titian's « Allegory of Religion »* in « Journal of the Warburg Institute ».

1951 - L. Vertova, *Tiziano*, Florence.

1952 - C. Nordenfalk, *Titian's Allegories on the Fondaco dei Tedeschi*, in « Gazette des Beaux-Arts ».

1952 - A. Lazzari, *Il ritratto del Mosti di Tiziano*, in «Arte Veneta».

1952 - W. Suida, *Miscellanea tizianesca*, I, in « Arte Veneta ».

1952 - 1953 R. Pallucchini, *Tiziano*, Lezioni universitarie, Bologna.

1953 - G. Fiocco, *Profilo di Francesco Vecellio*, in « Arte Veneta ».

1954 - G. Fiocco, *Il ritratto di Sperone Speroni dipinto da Tiziano*, in « Bollettino d'arte ».

1954 - A. Morassi, *Tiziano* in « Enciclopedia cattolica ».

1954 - A. Morassi, *Esordi di Tiziano*, in « Arte Veneta ».

1954 - E. Tietze Conrat, *Un soffitto di Tiziano a Brescia conservato in un disegno del Rubens*, in « Arte Veneta ».

1954 - F. Zeri, *La Galleria Spada*, Florence.

1955 - L. Baldass, *Eine Porträtskizze vom jungen Tizian*, in « Zeitschrift für Kunstwissenschaft ».

1955 - L. Coletti, *Tutta la pittura di Giorgione*, Milan.

1955 - P. Della Pergola, *Galleria Borghese, I dipinti*, catalogo, Rome.

1955 - G. A. Dell'Acqua, *Tiziano*, Milan.

1955 - G. Fiocco, *Profilo di Francesco Vecellio*, II, in « Arte Veneta ».

1955 - T. Pignatti, *Giorgione*, Milan.

1955 - T. Rousseau, *Tizian*, New York.

1955 - F. Valcanover, *Il polittico vecelliano di Sedico*, in « Archivio storico di Belluno, Feltre, e Cadore ».

1955 - P. Zampetti, *Giorgione e i Giorgioneschi*, Catalogo della Mostra, Venice.

1956 - G. Gamulin, *Un polittico di Tiziano nella cattedrale di Ragusa*, in « Venezia e l'Europa », Venice.

1956 - G. Fiocco, *A small portable panel by Titian for Philip II*, in « The Burlington Magazine ».

1956 - G. Fiocco, *Profilo di Francesco Vecellio*, III, in « Arte Veneta ».

1956 - A. Morassi, *Gli affreschi della Scuola del Santo a Padova*, Milan.

1956 - A. Morassi, *Ritratti del periodo giovanile di Tiziano*, in « Festschrift für A. Sas-Zaloziecky zum 60. Geburtstag », Graz.

1956 - E. Tietze Conrat, *Archeologia tizianesca*, in « Arte Veneta ».

1956 - W. Suida, *Miscellanea tizianesca*, II, in « Arte Veneta ».

1957 - B. Berenson, *Italian Pictures of the Renaissance, Venetian School*, Greenwich, Conn. and London.

1957 - U. Christoffel, *Tizian*, Stuttgart.

1958 - R. Pallucchini, *Un nuovo ritratto di Tiziano*, in « Arte Veneta ».

1959 - G. Fiocco, *La « Crocefissione » di Tiziano all'Escuriale e Orazio Vecellio*, in « Studies in the history of art dedicated to W. Suida », Greenwich, Conn., and London.

1959 - C. Gould, *The Sixteenth Century Venetian School*, Catalogo della Nat. Gall., London.

1960 - F. Valcanover, *Tutta la pittura di Tiziano*, Milan, 2 vol.

1960 - D. Frey, *Tizian und Michelangelo, zum Problem des Manierismus*, in « Museion », Studien aus Kunst u. Geschichte für O. H. Förster, Cologne.

1961 - R. Pallucchini, *Studi tizianeschi*, in « Arte Veneta ».

1961 - L. Baldass, *Zur Erforschung des « Giorgionismo » bei den Generationsgenossen Tizians*, in « Jahrbuch der Kunsth. Sammlungen in Wien ».

1962 - P. Hofer, *Die Pardo-Venus Tizians*, in « Festschrift Hans F. Hahnloser », Basel, Stuttgart.

1962 - A. Pope, *Titian's « Rape of Europe »*, London.

1964 - A. Morassi, *Tiziano*, « voce » in « Enciclopedia Universale dell'Arte ».

Plates

Plate 1

FÊTE CHAMPÊTRE. *Canvas, 43 ¼ x 54 ¼ in. (110 x 138 cm.); Paris, Louvre.*

Purchased by Charles I of England from the Duke of Mantua in 1627, the picture may have come from the collection of Isabella d'Este. Formerly in the possession of the French banker Jabach in 1649, it was added to the collection of Louis XIV in 1671.

This masterpiece has become famous not only for its intensely poetical quality but also because of the controversies which the question of its attribution has provoked in the art world. Some scholars still consider it a work by Giorgione; others, more open-minded, favor Titian; and still others have suggested that it might be a subject conceived by Giorgione and simply finished by Titian.

The traditional attribution to Giorgione was first contested in the 19th century, when the painting was erroneously ascribed to either Palma Vecchio or Sebastiano del Piombo and even to one of Sebastiano's followers. However, the argument that it might not be a work of Giorgione's late period but of Titian's youthful period continued to gain ground.

Although it has a good deal of Giorgione's subtle enchantment, this marvelous painting reveals, nonetheless, a new artistic conception which emphasizes the human figure, as do such authentic works of Titian's as the frescoes of the Scuola del Santo in Padua.

The *Fête Champêtre* should be dated ca. 1509-10, hence slightly earlier than Titian's frescoes in Padua where almost identical youthful figures appear.

Titian. *Self-portrait, detail.* Madrid, Prado. Canvas 33²/₄ x 25¹/₂ in. (86 x 65 cm.).

Plate 2

ST. ANTHONY GRANTING SPEECH TO AN INFANT. *Fresco, 126 x 124 in. (320 x 315 cm.); Padua, Scuola del Santo.*

One of the three frescoes commissioned to Titian at the Scuola del Santo in Padua in 1510, the year when Giorgione died of the plague in Venice.

The frescoes are the basis for reconstructing the œuvre of Titian's youthful period, since they constitute the first documented work of the artist after his participation in the frescoes of 1508 for the Fondaco dei Tedeschi.

Between April 23 and December 2, 1511, when he received the balance of his fee (the actual working time however must have been much shorter as the winter precludes any painting of murals), Titian furnished overwhelming proof of his talent and artistic capability, eclipsing (as Ridolfi justly remarked in 1648) any other painter who had ever worked there and giving a tremendous impetus to contemporary Venetian painting by his superiority. Such expressive power, such vigorous, emotional, vividly realistic interpretation of human events had never been seen before. In their artistic significance, these Padua frescoes are equalled only by Michelangelo's frescoes in the Sistine Chapel, begun in 1508, and by Raphael's frescoes of 1509 in the Stanza of the Vatican.

These frescoes in Padua were restored, rather negligently, by Francesco Zanon in 1748, and they are still in poor condition.

According to contemporary documents, Francesco Vecellio, Titian's older brother, also worked here at the same time. But his works are conspicuously inferior to the achievements of the master. Therefore we may dismiss the hypothesis that Francesco Vecellio notably influenced his brother's artistic education, except perhaps for some purely manual dexterity. (See Morassi, 1956.)

Plate 3

ST. ANTHONY GRANTING SPEECH TO AN INFANT, *detail of the head of the mother. Fresco, Scuola del Santo, Padua.*

This beautiful profile is indicative of the ideal of feminine beauty conceived by Titian in his youth. In the so-called *Portrait of a Slavonian Lady* in London we find the same type, even the same model, somewhat idealized in the fresco. In the color reproduction opposite we note the rhythm of the free, rapid brushstrokes which fuse together when seen from a distance.

Plate 4

THE CONCERT. *Canvas, 42½ x 48 in. (108 x 122 cm.); Florence, Pitti Palace.*

Acquired in Venice by Cardinal Ippolito de Medici in 1654 as a work by Giorgione and so recorded (1660) also by Boschini. Ridolfi (1648) saw the painting in the house of Paolo del Sera, a Florentine nobleman and art collector, and described it as " an Augustinian friar gracefully playing the harpsichord and turning his head to look at a round-faced friar clad in surplice and a black cape and holding a viola; on the other side is a youth wearing a hat adorned with white feathers. "
The painting is one of those traditionally ascribed to Giorgione's mature years but now recognized by scholars almost unanimously as a work of the young Titian to whom it was first attributed by Morelli. Though reminiscent of Giorgione in its suggestion of sustained enchantment borne by the lingering sounds of music of the harpsichord, the composition differs from the pictorial concepts of Giorgione by a more sharply defined humaneness and greater vitality which weld the three persons into a harmonious whole. The ascetic face of the harpsichord player recalls that of other portraits by Titian ca. 1510, and we may not be too far amiss in detecting here a resemblance with the features of Giorgione himself as they appear in the self-portrait in Braunschweig.

Plate 5-6

SACRED AND PROFANE LOVE. *Canvas, 46½ x 109¾ in. (118 x 279 cm.); Rome, Borghese Gallery.*

The painting may have come to the Borghese Gallery as one of seventy-one pictures which Scipione Borghese bought from Cardinal Sfondrato in 1608.

Here is one of Titian's most famous but also one of his most enigmatic works. The subject is as difficult to interpret as Giorgione's notably ambiguous compositions.

Mentioned by Ridolfi (1648) simply as " two women near a fountain, between them a little boy looking at his reflection in the water, " the picture has been given a wide variety of titles: *Beauty Adorned and Unadorned* (1613), *Three Loves* (1650), *Sacred and Profane Love* (1693), and others involving even literary and mythological themes such as *Polifilo and Polia* from F. Colonna's *Hypnerotomachia* (1499), and *Venus and Medea*. The painting has also been given romantic interpretations according to which the two women represent two aspects of Violante, the daughter of Palma Vecchio who was Titian's beloved. The title *Sacred and Profane Love* is the most commonly accepted.

Since the coat of arms with a sea monster and a rampant lion on the front of the fountain belongs to Nicolò Aurelio, Great Chancellor of Venice, the painting may be presumed to have been commissioned by him. If so, we have to dismiss A. Venturi's hypothesis (1928) that this famous work might be identical to the " bathing scene " which, according to one of his letters dated February 19, the artist had finished for Alfonso d'Este in 1517.

However, there has been no disagreement over the suggestive power of this work, whose figures pertinently described by Dolce (1557), appear " lifelike, moving, their bodies atremble. " In their enchantingly impressive reality they dominate a landscape subdued in tonality but echoing a profound, Giorgionesque lyricism.

This work, datable around 1515, has come to us in excellent condition, retaining even the black border around the scene, which all but touches the head and feet of the nude figure.

Plate 7

PORTRAIT OF A MUSICIAN. *Canvas, 39 x 32 ¼ in. (99 x 81.8 cm); Rome, Spada Gallery.*

The letters " C. A." on the parapet probably are the initials of the musician.
This portrait, perhaps unfinished, of a young cellist was believed to be that of " Messer Batista Ceciliano, excellent violinist, a very good work, " painted, according to Vasari, by Titian's son Orazio during his stay in Rome (1546). However, the masterful execution of the work precludes both its attribution to Orazio and its late dating. Attributed also to Giorgione (Hermanin) but reclaimed for Titian by Morassi (1942), Pallucchini (1953), and Zeri (1954), it was shown at the Giorgione Exhibition in Venice in 1955 as the work of Titian.
The keen individualization of the musician and the style of the painting link it with Titian's portraits of the early second decade, when Giorgione's influence still prevailed. The years 1515-1518 would seem to be its approximate date.

Plate 8

PORTRAIT OF A MAN WITH GLOVES. *Canvas, 39¼ x 35 in. (100 x 89 cm.); Paris, Louvre.*

Signed: TICIANUS F.

From the Gonzaga collection in Mantua, the painting passed to Charles I of England in 1627, and later from the collection of the French banker Jabach to Louis XIV.

This is one of the most famous and fascinating portraits of Titian's early period. From among the hypotheses advanced as to the identity of the man, we mention those of Hourticq (1919) and Mayer (1925). The former suggested one Gerolamo Adorno, deceased in 1523, whose portrait Titian sent to Federigo Gonzaga in 1527, together with that of Aretino's. Mayer believed the portrait represented Giambattista Malatesta, an agent of the Mantuan court in Venice.

The suggestive power of the portrait brings to mind the comments of Zanetti (1771) regarding Titian's heads in which " he concentrated mainly on the eyes, nose, and mouth, while confining himself to barely suggested, soft outlines elsewhere, thus producing an effect of liveliness and a reflection of the person's character in these heads."

Cavalcaselle (II, 425-26) mentioned a later copy of the portrait, signed "Titianus," in the Braunschweig Gallery.

The painting may be dated about 1520.

Plate 9

PORTRAIT OF VINCENZO MOSTI. *Canvas transferred to wood, 33 ½ x 26 in. (85 x 66 cm.); Florence, Pitti Palace.*

On the reverse of the panel is written " Thomaso Mosti, age 25 in the year 1526, Thitiano de Cadore, painter, " probably copied from an old inscription. Altered by early repainting, the portrait was erroneously considered a copy by Titian when still in the Leopoldo de Medici collection.

According to Cavalcaselle (I, 273), this portrait of Alfonso d'Este's confidant was begun in Venice but completed in Ferrara on the occasion of Titian's visit to the d'Este court, probably in November, 1524, or shortly thereafter.

Lazzari's research in 1952 established that the identification of the person with Tommaso Mosti is completely unfounded and much more probably that this is a portrait of Vincenzo Mosti, a nobleman at the court of Ferrara who was made a count in 1526 and died in 1536.

Because of its stylistic affinity with the *Man with Gloves* in the Louvre (Plate 8), the portrait has generally been dated in the early 1520's.

Plate 10

WORSHIP OF VENUS. *Canvas, 67 ¾ x 68 ¾ in. (172 x 175 cm.); Madrid, Prado.*

Picture is No. 102 in the Escorial.

Together with two Bacchanalian scenes in the Prado and in the National Gallery, London, this painting originally formed part of the decoration, begun in 1514, of Alfonso d'Este's chambers which, in addition to works by Dosso Dossi, contained Giovanni Bellini's famous *Feast of the Gods* (later restored by Titian), now in Washington. Titian's pictures were taken to the Ludovisi Palace in Rome by Cardinal Aldobrandini in 1598, and two of them, the *Worship of Venus* and the *Bacchanal* in the Prado, were presented to Philip IV of Spain through the Viceroy Monterey in 1639. The *Worship of Venus* was known to be at the Alcazar in 1666.

Mengs stated that when these three pictures were still in Rome, they were the object of intense study and admiration by Domenichino, Poussin and Albani; and Boschini (1660) mentioned that Domenichino wept at the thought of these paintings being taken to Spain.

We know from Titian's copious correspondence with the d'Este court that negotiations concerning the commission of the first of the three pictures were initiated by the Duke's agent in Venice, Jacopo Tebaldi. Alfonso d'Este then supplied the artist with the necessary materials of frame and canvas and informed him also of the subject chosen for the picture. Titian replied on April 1, 1518; but the work was somewhat delayed, and on September 29, 1519, the Duke wrote to Tebaldi, who hastened to assure his illustrious patron that Titian was on his way to Ferrara intending to complete the painting there. By the time he did so it was October 17, 1519.

The theme suggested by the Duke was taken from Philostratus' *Immagini* (Book IV, Erotes). In scrupulous adherence to the theme, Titian produced a powerful evocation of the classical myth " depicting charming and lovely children that reach the heart through the eyes . . . on a soft lawn of delicate leaves . . . all around them the delight of trees heavy with gold and ruby-colored apples, and aloft are cupids relieving the loaded branches of their sweet fruits which they toss down for the baskets of their companions; others still on the tree trunks, climbing their way to the top; and one is seen aiming an arrow from his bow at a friend whose breast is openly offered; still others using apples as missiles in a lively game, while some in kissing vie with each other in a scene of love . . . " (Ridolfi, 1648). Truly a hymn to life swelled by the joyful chorus of nature!

Tietze dated the painting 1515-18 while Gronau suggested a date prior to 1516. There is no valid argument against the hypothesis, now generally considered acceptable, that this is the first of the Bacchanalian scenes which according to extant documents was commissioned and executed by Titian between April, 1518, and October, 1519.

The museum in Stockholm owns a freely interpreted copy of this picture by Rubens.

Plate 12

A BACCHANAL (THE PEOPLE OF ANDROS), *detail. Madrid, Prado.*

Tietze has pointed to the figure of the youth leaning on one arm, next to the Bacchante raising a bowl, as being derived directly from Michelangelo's drawing for the *Battle of the Cascina,* now in the Leicester collection at Holkham Hall. It is quite possible that Titian might have seen a fragment of Michelangelo's *Battle* done ca. 1515-16 in a collection in Mantua in the 16th century.

For further details on the painting see the notes to Plate 11.

Plate 13

DEPOSITION. *Canvas, 58 ¼ x 88 ½ in. (148 x 225 cm.); Paris, Louvre.*

The painting was among the art treasures in Mantua assembled by Gonzaga, which were sold by Vincenzo Gonzaga. In 1628 the picture was in the possession of Charles I of England and displayed in the first room of the King's private suite at Whitehall. After the death of Charles I, the work was bought for one hundred twenty pounds sterling by the French banker Jabach, from whom it went into the collection of Louis XIV.

Although not mentioned in Federigo Gonzaga's correspondence, the *Deposition* is generally believed to have been painted for the Marquis of Mantua, or for his mother, Isabella d'Este, around the mid-1520's.

Titian's relations with Gonzaga began in 1523. In a letter dated January 25, Giambattista Malatesta, Federigo's agent in Venice, mentioned " Maestro Ticiano, an excellent artist, modest and kind in every respect. " Desirous of enlisting the service of the then already famous artist, on February 3, 1523, Gonzaga approached Alfonso d'Este, for whom the artist was executing the third and last Bacchanalian scene, with the request that he allow Titian to paint for him " a work which I want him to do, and which will take only a few days, " presumably a portrait (Cavalcaselle, I, 248-49).

It has been pointed out that the *Deposition* suggests Raphael's version of the same subject, now in the Borghese Gallery, Rome. Even though there may be echoes of Raphael in parts of Titian's composition, our painting is much more dramatic in its impact by virtue of its more intense and effective use of color.

The painting was later enlarged by the addition of a strip of canvas to its upper part in the ill-conceived notion of giving the composition more breathing space; whereas it was the artist's explicit intention to emphasize the grandiose effect of his towering figures by confining them to the narrowness of a restricted space (as also in *Sacred and Profane Love*). Numerous engravings were made after this painting by Rousselet, Chaperon, Masson, De Marc, Filhol, and Landon. Cavalcaselle mentioned a copy in the size of the original, perhaps by one of the master's followers, at one time in the Manfrin collection in Venice.

Plate 14

MADONNA OF THE PESARO FAMILY, *detail of a girl. Venice, Sta. Maria dei Frari.*

Among the members of the Pesaro family headed by Jacopo, Bishop of Paphus, who commissioned the altarpiece, we notice this lifelike portrait of a girl whose intent glance at the spectator is both human and divine.

For the history of the painting installed in 1526 on the Altar of the Conception in the Church of the Frari, which also contained Titian's *Assumption,* see the notes on Figure 11.

Plate 16

THE PRESENTATION OF THE VIRGIN, *central part. Canvas, 139¾ x 305 in. (345 x 775 cm.); Venice, Academy.*

The picture, painted for the Brotherhood of Saint Mary of Charity in 1534-38, once decorated a wall of the hostelry-room in the Scuola della Carità which is now a part of the Academy. When two doors were later broken through the wall, the painting had to be trimmed on either side. It was cleaned in the 18th century and the sky was found to be in poor condition (Zanetti, 1771). In the 19th century it was enlarged by ten centimeters both above and below by the painter Sebastiano Santi, who also restored it in parts.

The composition, the largest one yet undertaken by Titian, follows in the tradition of Giovanni Bellini to some extent, but Titian has introduced elements from the local scene of his day, and set it against the background of the towering peaks of his native Marmarolian range. Among the group on the left are a number of actual portraits of Venetian senators (who partake in the ceremony dressed as the Pharisees), two of whom Ridolfi (1648) identified as the Great Chancellor, Andrea de' Franceschi, repeatedly portrayed by the artist, and Lazzaro Crasso.

The complexity of the scene is alleviated somewhat by the landscape in the background, the " large cloud almost in the center which, shining brightest, actually seems to move, to change its form, and to dissolve under the spectator's eyes " (Zanetti, 1771); while " the old peasant woman " in the foreground reminiscent of Carpaccio, " in rustic clothes, with eggs and chickens in a basket " (Ridolfi, 1648) adds a masterful touch of naturalism.

Plate 17

PORTRAIT OF A WOMAN ("LA BELLA"). *Canvas, 39 ¼ x 29 ½ in. (100 x 75 cm.); Florence, Pitti Palace.*

The painting came to the Medici collection from the Duke of Urbino as part of the patrimony of Vittoria della Rovere, the wife of Ferdinand II, in 1631.

This picture, one of Titian's most famous portraits, most probably is " that portrait of the lady in the blue dress " to which Francesco Maria della Rovere, Duke of Urbino, referred in his letter of May 2, 1536 to Leonardi, his agent in Venice, and which he wanted to have provided with a painted shutter used in those days to protect highly valuable paintings (" we want it to be finished well in every respect, and with a shutter ").

The same model, who must have appealed to Titian as an ideal of feminine beauty, sat also for the *Young Woman with a Fur* of the Kunsthistorisches Museum, Vienna, the *Young Woman with a Feather Hat*, in the Hermitage, Leningrad, and the *Venus of Urbino*. The identification of the model with Isabella d'Este or with Eleonora Gonzaga, Duchess of Urbino, is unfounded.

Plate 19

DANAE. *Canvas, 27 x 46 in. (69 x 117 cm.); Naples, Capodimonte Gallery.*

The painting formed part of the Farnese collection at the Palace of the Garden in Parma until 1680 when it was listed in its inventory. Titian had worked for the Farnese before his visit to Rome, painting for them the portrait of the young Ranuccio Farnese in 1541-2 (Washington, National Gallery), a portrait of Paul III, the family's most illustrious member (Naples, Capodimonte Gallery) during the Pope's stay at Busseto near Cremona for a meeting with Charles V in 1543, and other members of the powerful family. When the Farnese renewed their invitation to Rome in 1545, he accepted with the permission of Guidobaldo of Urbino, to whom he was deeply beholden at the time. Following a brief stay in Pesaro, he arrived in Rome in October accompanied by his son Orazio and an escort provided by the Duke of Urbino.

It must have been Ottavio Farnese, who was not an ecclesiastic, who commissioned the *Danae.* Vasari said that when visiting Titian at the Belvedere with Michelangelo one day, " they saw a painting, then in work, of a nude woman representing a Danae with Jupiter in the shape of a rain of gold, which (as is proper in the artist's presence) they praised highly; after they had taken their leave, discussing Titian's work, Michelangelo commended it greatly, stating that while he liked his coloring and manner very much, it seemed a pity that drawing was not taught properly in Venice . . . . " The quotation better reflects Vasari's taste than Michelangelo's since Vasari's style adhered to the mannerist conception of linear treatment of the figure.

After the *Venus of Urbino* Titian's beautiful women are endowed with a growing voluptuous liveliness, increasingly conscious of the space in which they are situated. Even so, the idealism of the figures and the mythical vehicle of the subject triumph over the sensuality and earthly flavor of the painting. Among the other important versions of *Danae,* a popular subject frequently chosen by Titian, we may mention those in the Prado and in Leningrad, both of a later date, and also the one in Vienna.

Plate 20

VENUS AND THE ORGAN-PLAYER AND CUPID. *Canvas, 58 ¼ x 85 ¼ in. (148 x 217 cm.); Madrid, Prado.*

Signed: TITIANUS F.

The painting was at the Alcazar in 1636 where it was damaged in the fire of 1734. From 1796 to 1827, the canvas was on display at the Madrid Academy with *Venus and Adonis* (see Figure 20); it came to the Prado in 1936.

The work has been identified with the *Venus* which Titian either painted in Augsburg, or brought with him from Venice for Granvelle, chancellor of Charles V, in 1548. In 1540 Nicolò Granvelle had completed the building of a palace in Besançon which — with the assistance of his son, Cardinal Antonio — he filled with precious art treasures: paintings by Correggio, Dürer, Paris Bordone, and especially Leonardo's *Mona Lisa*, as well as many works by Titian with whom the Granvelles maintained friendly and lasting relations. Titian's portrait of Nicolò Granvelle is in Besançon and that of Antonio Granvelle is in the Nelson Gallery in Kansas City. A descendent, the Count of Cantecroix, sold many pictures from their collection to Rudolph II in 1660, among them Titian's *Sleeping Venus with a Satyr* and *Venus with an Organ-Player*, the present painting. Other works by Titian, which are not easily identified today, went to Cantecroix's heirs: two portraits of the Chancellor; a portrait of his wife Nicolina Bonvalot; *Cupid Holding a Mirror for Venus*; a *Rain of Gold* or *Danae*; a *Lady Dressing*; a *Lady Seated*; a *Large Head*; and a *Young Boy* (Granvelle's *Inventory*, 1607, published by A. Caston, Monographie du Palais Granvelle à Besançon, 1867). Rudolph II later sent the *Venus and an Organ-Player* to Philip of Spain.

The fact that the *Venus*, like the *Danae*, was one of Titian's favorite subjects was confirmed by the painter himself in some of his letters to Charles V, one from Rome dated December 18, 1545, another of September, 1548, in which he referred to a " Venus of rare quality, almost lifelike " which he intended to present to the Emperor. Ridolfi, however, mentioned another painting for Francesco Assonica, done in Venice and later taken to England which some have identified with the Prado picture (53 ½ x 86 ½ in. / 136 x 220 cm., no. 420). There are many versions of this subject: the second example in the Prado includes a small dog; a picture in Berlin; a Venus without the organ player at the Uffizi; the *Venus with a Lute Player* in the Metropolitan Museum, New York, which is almost identical to the version at the Fitzwilliam Museum in Cambridge. In some of these works we clearly note the contribution of assistants.

Scholars like Tietze, Gronau, and Berenson believed they detected the hands of assistants in the Prado version, while Cavalcaselle (II, 106) doubted its authenticity altogether. However, the high quality of the execution in this work excludes any doubts of this kind. (Incidentally, Suida and Pallucchini both believe the painting to be by the master's own hand.)

Some copies of *Venus and an Organ-Player* are said to represent Philip II playing the organ in the presence of his paramour.

The classical subject of Venus is imbued with human warmth; rather than a goddess, Venus appears to be a woman well aware of her charms, relaxing happily before an idyllic landscape containing deer and peacocks as she listens to the gentle sound of organ music.

Plate 21

THE ALLOCUTION OF ALFONSO D'AVALOS, MARQUIS DEL VASTO. *Canvas, 87 ¾ x 65 in. (223 x 165 cm.); Madrid, Prado.*

The painting kept at the Alcazar in the time of Philip IV (1621), was mentioned in the inventory of the Escorial of 1666 where it suffered damage by fire in 1671, and later again at the Alcazar in 1734. A similar painting, if not the same, was among those which went from Mantua to the court of Charles I of England in Whitehall. The Prado catalogue (1942, p. 647) specifies that the Madrid version was acquired for 250 pounds at an auction sale of the collection of Charles I.

The work was commissioned by Alfonso d'Avalos, Marquis of Vasto and Pescara, probably in 1539 during his stay in Venice on the occasion of the election of the Doge Pietro Lando. When the patron complained about the delay in the delivery of the painting, Aretino offered apologies on behalf of the painter in a letter dated November 20, 1540, stating not quite truthfully that the " portrait had progressed admirably, the armor shining and the boy (the Marquis' son Francesco Ferrante) resembling Apollo by the side of Mars." However, a month later, on December 22, d'Avalos had to accept " a small-sized painting " sent by Titian " in order that . . . its beauty may please the eyes until the large canvas would be furnished, which will be shortly indeed, " as Aretino had written. He was speaking of an oil-sketch of the actual composition for the painting of which, through Aretino on February 15, 1541, Titian had asked Girolamo Martinengo of Brescia for a complete set of armor to be copied faithfully. Finally completed in August, 1541, the *Allocution* reached Alfonso d'Avalos in Milan where Charles V happened to be present, and according to Marcolini (Ticozzi, 1817, 122) the whole city " flocked together to admire it as a divine, most worthy image." We know from Ridolfi (1648) that the painting earned Titian an annual pension of fifty *scudi*. According to tradition Titian is said to have painted Aretino among the soldiers. Nothing is known about the small sketch for the large Prado canvas.

Plate 22

SAINT JOHN THE BAPTIST. *Canvas, 79 x 52¾ in. (201 x 134 cm.); Venice, Academy.*

Signed: TICIANUS

Mentioned by Dolce (1557), Vasari (1568), and Ridolfi (1648), as in the Church of Santa Maria Maggiore in Venice and subsequently removed, the painting might have been executed originally for that church.

Mayer's suggested date of 1530-32 for this work has since been modified to a more plausible 1540-45. There is little probability in Hourticq's suggestion (1930) that Titian might have been inspired by an engraving by Campagnola. It is obvious that the Mannerist conception of the figure is derived from the sculpture of Sansovino.

Titian followed the traditional iconography of the hermit saint. Ridolfi describes the figure " with unkempt hair, emaciated from fasting and prolonged penitence, clad in coarse camel hide in scorn of the purple and fine linens worn by arrogant mortals." However, the figure of Saint John is far from ascetic; it has the power of sculpture in the round, set against a landscape of rocks and woods with a silvery waterfall. The gesture of his hand suggests that he is preaching to a crowd of people. An engraving by Galgano Cipriani was included in Francesco Zanotto's work.

Plate 23

PORTRAIT OF THE SO-CALLED YOUNG ENGLISHMAN. *Canvas 43½ x 37¾ in. (111 x 96 cm.); Florence, Pitti Palace.*

The painting came to Florence from Urbino in 1631 as part of the estate of Vittoria della Rovere, the wife of Ferdinand II.

Listed in old inventories as a portrait of the Duke of Norfolk, the painting became known later as the portrait of a " Young Englishman. " Venturi suggested in 1928 that the sitter might be Ippolito Riminaldi, an attorney at the court in Ferrara, basing his hypothesis on a portrait of Ippolito in the Academy of St. Luke in Rome which is not by Titian's hand. Fogolari (1935) called the painting " Gentleman with the Haunting Eyes, " while Gronau suggested that it was a portrait of Guidobaldo II, Duke of Urbino, with whom Titian was known to have been in contact from 1538 to 1545. The style of the painting would indicate a date around 1540-45, now generally accepted by scholars. In any case the portrait with its subtle characterization is one of Titian's best.

Plate 24

POPE PAUL III AND HIS NEPHEWS, ALESSANDRO AND OTTAVIO FARNESE. *Canvas, 83 ¾ x 68 ½ in. (210 x 174 cm.); Naples, Capodimonte Gallery.*

The painting came to the gallery in Naples from the Palace of the Garden in Parma; in the Farnese inventory of 1680, it is listed as a " sketch " (see Campori, *Raccolta di Cataloghi*, Modena, 1870, 273). Upon his arrival in Rome in 1545, Vasari reported that Titian " having rested a few days was assigned rooms at the Belvedere in order that he might paint another portrait of Pope Paul and that of Farnese and the Duke Ottavio; these he executed admirably and to the great satisfaction of these gentlemen." The emotional impact of this astounding group, unsurpassed as a prototype for much of portrait painting in the 16th and 17th centuries, evolves around the figure of the aging Pope sunk back in his armchair, yet throbbing with vitality, and his imperious face with its sharp penetrating eyes. Through his inherent energy and determination we are made aware of the emotions which animate these three figures.

The broad style, almost sketchy in parts, which foreshadows the painter's late style, has led to the assumption that for some unknown reason the painting was not finished.

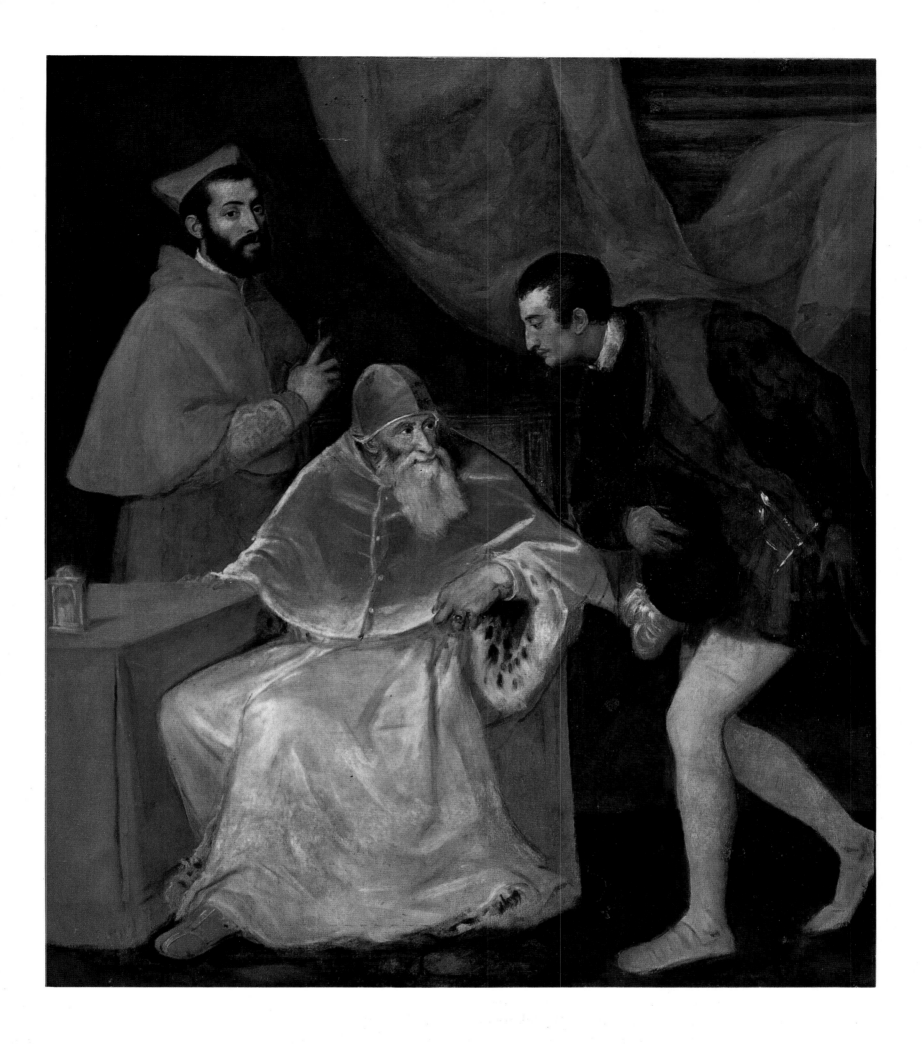

Plate 25

PAUL III WITH HIS NEPHEWS, *detail from the preceding plate; Naples, Capodimonte Gallery.*

At the period of their first contact with Titian, the Farnese family was powerful, dominating the politics of the time through Paul III who maneuvered cleverly between Francis I and Charles V. Triumphant at the Council of Trent in 1545, the Pope had then invested Pier Luigi Farnese with the dukedom of Parma and Piacenza, and promoted his nephews Alessandro and Ranuccio to the rank of cardinal. His efforts to obtain from Charles V the dukedom of Milan for Ottavio, however, had been unsuccessful.

Titian arrived in Rome at a moment when the Farnese were involved in dynastic struggles. Ottavio, the son of Pier Luigi and husband of Margaret of Austria, daughter of Charles V, resented his father's acquisition of the dukedom of Parma and Piacenza through Paul III. Supported by the Emperor, he complained to the Pope without success.

Cavalcaselle remarked (II, 63) that from the lifelike way Paul III turns abruptly to his nephew with scornful reproval it may be deduced that Titian actually witnessed such a scene. Titian had free access to the papal suite when lodging at the Belvedere. Ottavio may have taken offense at the picture and prevented its completion. In this detail we note plainly the mature Titian's way of painting in patches and short impetuous brushstrokes by which he achieved an intensity of color and light effects never before realized.

Plate 26

VOTIVE PORTRAIT OF THE VENDRAMIN FAMILY, *detail. Canvas, 81 x 118½ in (206 x 301 cm.); London, National Gallery.*

A painting probably commissioned by the Vendramin family. Andrea, an ancestor, guardian of the School of St. John the Evangelist, in 1369 had received the relic of the True Cross, in this work adored on the altar (Figure 18) by the assembled family (Pouncey, 1939).

The picture was once believed to represent the Cornaro family and dated ca. 1560 (Cavalcaselle, II, 273). Gronau (1925), on the other hand, who identified the group as members of the Vendramin family, proposed a date ca. 1550, based on Gabriel's death in 1552. We have yet an earlier date of ca. 1547, as archival research has disclosed that Andrea and Leonardo Vendramin died in 1547, the year in which Gabriel drew up his last will (see Gould, 1959; Valcanover, 1960). Gould also suggested that the painting may have been started about 1543 and completed later.

The three boys, grouped on the altar steps in this detail, are Federico, Fillipo, and Giovanni Vendramin.

After the *Portrait of Paul III and his Nephews,* Titian created in this family group a new masterpiece in which each figure is a highly personalized character study. The little boys on the right are shown in their natural liveliness, hardly impressed by the solemnity of the moment. The youngsters to the left form a more serious and composed trio. Between them in austere dignity the family patriarchs bend with deep devotion before the ancient sacred relic. And to illuminate the entire scene in its impressive grandeur, there are only two candles on either side of the Greek cross on the unadorned altar, rendered in a stippled, summary and " impressionist " manner which anticipates the painter's late style.

For further details on the painting see the notes to Figure 18.

Plate 27

PORTRAIT OF PRINCE PHILIP OF SPAIN. *Canvas, 73½ x 39¼ in. (187 x 100 cm.); Naples, Capodimonte Gallery.*

Signed: TITIANUS EQUES CAES. F.

The picture was listed as part of Odoardo Farnese's estate at Caprarola in 1626. It went to the Palace of the Garden in Parma from the Farnese Palace in Rome in 1652, and probably was taken to Naples together with other works of art by Charles III in 1698.

On the reverse of a letter which Titian addressed to Philip on March 23, 1553, the Prince acknowledged, June 18, that through Vargas, the servant of the Spanish Ambassador in Venice, he had received his portrait, and expressed " infinite thanks for the care bestowed on this commission " (Archive of Simancas, Leg. 1336; Cavalcaselle, II, 236). The picture referred to in that letter is generally believed to be the one illustrated here. However, both Tietze and Mayer (1925) consider the Naples portrait an excellent workshop copy of the original sent to Spain and now believed lost. Yet the high quality of the painting and its great nobility, characteristic of some of Titian's portraits of that period and attributable in part to examples of German art which the painter had had an opportunity to see during his stay in Augsburg (1548; 1550-51), both point to Titian as the artist.

The version in the Pitti Palace however is a workshop copy, certainly the one which was seen by Vasari together with the portrait of Charles V in the collection of the Grand Duke Cosimo I. Another portrait of Prince Philip shown in three-quarter length (National Gallery, Rome) is probably a workshop copy of a lost original which inspired also the portrait in the Prado attributed to Sanchez Coello (Mayer, 1925).

A full-length portrait of Philip in armor, done by Titian in Augsburg in 1551, is likewise in the Prado.

Plate 28

VENUS OF PARDO, *detail. Canvas, 77 x 151½ in. (196 x 385 cm.); Paris, Louvre.*

The painting was named for the Pardo Palace in Madrid where it was housed until 1624, and known to have been damaged in a fire in 1608. It was presented to Charles of England by Philip IV of Spain on his visit to the British court to ask for the hand of the Stuart King's sister. In 1650-51 the painting was bought by Jabach in London for six hundred pound sterling and later valued at ten thousand tournois in the inventory of Cardinal Mazarin's collection from which it eventually passed to Louis XIV. Prior to the 17th century nothing is known about the history of this painting which represents "Antiope Surprised by Jupiter in the Disguise of a Satyr." In addition to the identification already suggested (see notes Figure 15), we may recall that a *Sleeping Venus with a Satyr* was among the various pictures which a descendant of Granvelle, Chancellor of Charles V, sold to Rudolf II in 1660 (see note to Plate 20). The dating has always been problematic, varying between ca. 1560 (Fogolari), 1535-40 (Tietze), and the early 1540's (Pallucchini, 1953); others have considered it one of Titian's early compositions which he may have resumed painting at a later date (Hofer, 1962). Here is a work of great artistic balance whose poetic harmony of landscape and figures recall those of the Bacchanalian scenes, but whose more fluid style places it closer to the "poetic subjects" painted for Philip II ca. 1560. Disfigured by poor repainting in 1661, the work has undergone various changes in the course of time. Among other things, it was restored by Antonio Coypel and transferred to a new canvas in 1829.

Plate 29

THE EDUCATION OF CUPID. *Canvas, 46½ x 72¾ in. (118 x 185 cm.); Rome, Borghese Gallery.*

Mentioned by Ridolfi (1648) who calls it *The Graces with Cupid* " in the residence of Prince Borghese " in Rome, together with the *Sacred and Profane Love*, this work probably came to the Borghese Gallery as one of the acquisitions by Scipione Borghese in 1608 from Cardinal Sfondrato. It was listed in the catalogue of the Gallery in 1613 as *The Three Graces*.

Generally dated in the mid-1560's, the work is one of the masterpieces painted in Titian's declining years. The style expresses a new essence of reality transformed. If, as Vasari states, the paintings made by Titian in his youth were " refined and painstaking, " those of his old age are very different, for they are " executed in heavy, boldly applied brushstrokes and patches, clearly discernible from nearby, but appearing perfect when seen at a distance." Vasari's visit to Venice in 1566 provided an opportunity for him to see the paintings then in the process of execution in Titian's studio. At that time Titian's art was no longer concerned with " making the flowers look prettier, the grass more shining, the plants more sprightly, the birds more endearing, the animals more graceful, and the humans more stately " (Ridolfi). Instead he was now probing the innermost substance of nature itself.

Plate 30

THE EDUCATION OF CUPID, *detail. Rome, Borghese Gallery.*

The subject is one that Titian preferred in his youth, but now his painting style is entirely different. This was well expressed by Cavalcaselle (II, 343-44) who says " one sees only a confusion of massive brushstrokes of red, turquois and black with occasional admixtures of gray and blue, in a technique which one might call loose, and the forms indefined in contours; but when seen at a proper distance the picture suddenly becomes transformed, taking on forms and colors which all but match nature itself."

Plate 31

PORTRAIT OF JACOPO STRADA. *Canvas, 49 ¼ x 37 ¼ in. (125 x 95 cm.); Vienna, Kunsthistorisches Museum.*

Signed: TITIANUS F.

Mentioned by Boschini as being in the gallery of Archduke Leopold of Austria, who had acquired it in 1659, the painting went to the imperial collection after Leopold's death.

On the table covered by a green cloth we note a marble torso, antique coins and a letter addressed to " Mag(nifi)co Sig(no)r Titian Vecellio...Venezia. " A cartouche in the upper right-hand corner bears the following inscription: IACOBUS DE STRADA. CIVIS. ROMANUS. CAESS. ANTIQUARIUS. ET. COM. BELIC. AN: AETAT: LI et C.M.D. L. XVI.

It is the portrait of the Mantuan (later Roman citizen) Jacopo Strada, one of the most famous and proficient antiquarians of his day and well-known by the illustrious and wealthy. He was appointed Imperial Antiquarian and entered the service of the court of Bavaria. Protected by Fugger and assisted by Bernardo Olgiati, Castellino, and Nicolò Stoppio to whom he turned over his business when leaving for Bavaria, Strada was in frequent contact with Titian for estimates and sales of art objects. In 1566 Titian got in touch with him for the purchase of pictures, engravings and antique sculptures which were to be added to the collection of Albert V of Bavaria. (For Titian's interesting relations with antiquarians and art dealers, see Stockbauer, *Kunstbestrebungen am Bayerischen Hof*, where Stoppio's letters and Strada's activities are published). According to Zimmermann (*Mitteilungen des Instituts für Oesterreichische Geschichtsforschung, Erganzungsband*, VI), Strada's portrait was begun in 1567 and completed in 1568. Since it is Titian's last known dated painting, it enables us to see the painter's stylistic and conceptual development· by comparing it with his Giorgionesque portraits. It is executed with " forceful strokes of thick color " (Boschini, 1647) restricted to essential and significant elements as is characteristic of Titian's late style.

Plate 32

THE ENTOMBMENT. *Canvas, 54 x 68¾ in. (137 x 175 cm.); Madrid, Prado (no. 440).*

Signed: TITIANUS VECELLIUS AEQUES CAES.

In a letter of July 13, 1559, from Ghent, Philip II recommended special care in the shipment of two
" poetical subjects, " *Diana and Callisto* and *Diana and Actaeon,* commissioning him at the same time
to paint another " Christ in the Sepulchre " to replace the one done in 1557 and lost at Trento on
its way to Spain. On August 3, 1559, the King's secretary, Hernandez, informed Philip that in addition
to the two above-mentioned " poetical paintings " Titian had sent him also an *Entombment* that was
" larger in size than the previous version, its figures being executed in full length; and a small
imaginative picture representing a Turkish or Persian girl, all perfectly executed " (Cavalcaselle, II,
244). The painting was sent to Genoa in September of the same year as announced to the King on
September 27 by Titian who also expressed his satisfaction that it " turned out to be superior to
the first;" and he attributed " its improvement largely to my dismay at the loss of the first picture."
The *Entombment* remained on the altar of the Royal Chapel of Aranjuez until 1574, and subsequently
was placed in the old church of the Escorial until it went to the Prado in 1837. A slightly different,
later copy is also in the Prado (No. 441).

As in Titian's *Entombment* in the Louvre, the sacred, dramatic scene is restricted in space and lives only
through its figures which appear as if expanded in their sublime grandeur. The emotional impact of
the *Entombment* is intensified by the bold, almost violently applied strokes of color.

Plate 33

ANNUNCIATION. *Canvas, 148 ½ x 92 ½ in. (403 x 235 cm.); Venice, Church of S. Salvatore.*

Signed beneath the prayer stool: TITIANUS FECIT FECIT.

In his comments on the work, Ridolfi (1648) said " since the owners of the picture felt that it did not equal Titian's other work in perfection, the artist added the second *fecit* to his signature in order to remind them of their lack of understanding." Tietze believed the second *" fecit "* was added by a restorer and that it covers the date of the painting. The validity of his hypothesis has not been verified.

Since the *Annunciation* was mentioned also by Vasari, who was in Venice in 1566, we may believe it was finished shortly prior to that year. Regarding this painting and the *Transfiguration* in S. Salvatore, Vasari writes: " Although we can see some good aspects in these last works, they are not greatly valued by him (Titian), and they lack the perfection which distinguishes his other paintings." In this painting Titian has resumed the composition which he had executed in 1557 or shortly afterwards for the Church of S. Domenico Maggiore in Naples, but he has surpassed it in dramatic, pictorial vision. This way of painting was so different from the accepted norms of artistic expression that it could not fail to upset critics and connoisseurs, including, as we have seen, also Vasari. Nevertheless, it is difficult to understand the exact meaning of Vasari's phrase, " they are not greatly valued by him."

Plate 34

ANNUNCIATION, *detail of Angel's head. Venice, Church of S. Salvatore.*

While in the handling of the Madonna's head Titian adhered largely to a traditional style in terms of careful drawing and refined plasticity, the head of the angel seems a visionary image conceived in violent frenzied strokes, and emerging through the ardor of the creative process.

Plate 35

ADAM AND EVE. *Canvas, 94 ½ x 73 ¼ in. (240 x 186 cm.); Madrid, Prado.*

Signed: TITIANUS F.

The painting is not mentioned in Titian's correspondence with the Spanish court. In the 17th century it was all but forgotten in the sacristy of the Royal Chapel in Madrid. It miraculously escaped complete destruction in the Alcazar fire of 1734, in which it was damaged however, and substantially restored by Juan de Miranda.

Generally dated ca. 1560-70, the composition recalls previous formal arrangements, reminiscent of Michelangelo for its conspicuous plasticity. It has been suggested that Titian may have returned to a work begun much earlier (Pallucchini, 1953). Sanchez-Canton, on the other hand, has pointed out (1942) that Titian may have had in mind an etching by Dürer.

During his visit to Spain in 1628-29, Rubens painted a free interpretation of this work (now also in the Prado, No. 1692). Boschini (1660, 336) reported that shortly before his death Titian began another version of this subject which he was unable to finish, completing only the figure of Eve. Nothing is known about the present whereabouts of this painting, once owned by the prosecutor Morosini, in which the figure of Adam was completed by Tintoretto, the landscape by Ludovico Pozzo of Treviso (probably the artist called Pozzoserrato), and a number of animals by Bassano.

Plate 36

RELIGION DEFENDED BY SPAIN. *Canvas, 66 x 66 in. (168 x 168 cm.); Madrid, Prado.*

Signed: TITIANUS F.

Generally identified as the painting which Titian began for Alfonso I d'Este but left unfinished in his studio after the Duke's death in 1534. The picture, seemingly intended to represent the " Triumph of Virtue over Vice, " was described by Vasari who saw it in the artist's studio during his short visit to Venice in 1566: " a nude girl bowing to Minerva accompanied by another figure, and the sea with Neptune in a chariot in the background."

Titian probably returned to this compositional scheme after the battle of Lepanto, adapting it to the new subject extolling the Spanish victory over the infidels. On September 24, 1575, the artist was ready to ship both this painting and the *Allegory of the Battle of Lepanto* to Philip II.

An old copy, slightly different and unfinished, 66 x 67 ¾ in. (168 x 172 cm.), in the Doria Gallery in Rome was believed erroneously (Tietze-Conrat, 1951) to have been the model for the painting which Titian did for Alfonso d'Este and might have returned for the Madrid version, and also for another one, now lost, offered to Maximilian II, which was engraved by G. Fontana and mentioned in the Emperor's correspondence of 1568 with his representative in Venice.

Madrazo (Catalogue, 1872, p. 266) stated that Titian had duplicated the subject for the Doria family, who had contributed substantially to the victory of Lepanto, painting their coat of arms on the shield held by the figure representing Religion. However, there is no trace of the Doria insignia in the painting in the Doria Gallery.

Plate 37

SHEPHERD AND NYMPH. *Canvas, 55 ¾ x 73 ½ in. (142 x 187 cm.); Vienna, Kunsthistorisches Museum.*

Once in the collection of Archduke Leopold William (1659), this admirable painting has been tentatively identified (Tietze, 1950) as *Diana and Endymion* supposedly offered by Titian to Maximilian II in 1568.

It has been suggested that the nymph might have been inspired by a nude in Giulio Campagnola's engraving of a work by Giorgione; which would mean that Titian in one of his last works returned to the pastoral theme of his youth, now, however, conceived and expressed in an altogether different pictorial language. The scene seems to be set in a world barely emerging from chaos and flame and still alive with primordial energy. Adolfo Venturi (1928) furnished a masterful interpretation of this work of art: " In the summery dusk of the open countryside, a nymph reclines on the hide of a wild beast. Behind her, the shepherd lowers his flute to pause for a look at the forest maiden whom he has just eulogized in a hymn, and to bring his garland-clad head closer to the voluptuous beauty who turns her head as if aware of being watched. There is sensuousness in the air and in the light, crowning a sun-filled day, which, spreading downward in flakes of semi-solid matter, seems to engulf the torrid earth as if in a layer of incandescent ashes."

A copy of the painting by Palma the Younger in the Museo Civico, Treviso, shows additions on either side which are missing in the original. This confirms Tietze's and Jedlicka's conjectures that the picture in Vienna was mutilated. A work to be dated early in the 1570's.

Plate 38

TARQUINIUS AND LUCREZIA. *Canvas. 55" x 39 ¼" in. (140 x 100 cm.); Vienna, Academy of Fine Arts.*

The picture, offered at the Schroff sale of 1907, was acquired by the Academy of Fine Arts in Vienna. The fact that it had to be withdrawn subsequently from exhibition because of harsh criticism by both artists and experts reveals the lack of understanding as late as the beginning of this century which surrounded the works of Titian's final style. When it was published by Bode (in *Kunstchronik* N. F. XXVII N. 2) as one of Titian's masterpieces, the painting was placed on exhibition once again.
The work is one of the most perfect expressions of the master's late style. A more " descriptive " version of the subject was executed for Philip II and shipped to him in 1571 (now in the Fitzwilliam Museum, Cambridge).
A painting of *Tarquinius and Lucrezia* was mentioned by the Anonymous Tizianello (1622) in the possession of Count Arundel, who donated it to Charles I of England (Ridolfi, 1648). From there it went to France and eventually found its way into the collection of Louis XIV (1661). In 1752-54 this work was listed in Lépicié's catalogue of the Louvre (Catalogue raisonné 1754). In 1804 it was in the Museum of Bordeaux where it was severely damaged in the fire of 1870. It has since disappeared from sight.
The Vienna version must be assigned to Titian's last years ca. 1570-76.

Plate 39

PIETÀ. *Canvas, 138 ¼ x 153" in. (351 x 389 cm.); Venice, Academy.*

Ridolfi reported (1648) that Titian had begun to paint a picture with the dead Saviour resting at the breast of His grieving Mother, supported by Saint Jerome, and the Magdalene with arms outspread in profound grief. Titian intended it to go to the Chapel of the Frari who had given permission to have the painting hung; but because of the delay in completing this work, or because of their reluctance to relinquish an ancient Crucifix kept there, it was left unfinished and inherited after the master's death by Palma who completed it, adding a few small angels and the following humble inscription: " Quod Titianus inchoatum reliquit/ Palma reverenter perfict/ Deoque dicavit opus. " Recent research has confirmed that Titian's unfinished altarpiece at the Academy was actually completed by Palma the Younger.

After Titian's death the *Pietà* was first installed in the church of Sant'Angelo and later taken to the Academy.

It has been reported (Cavalcaselle, II, 410) that the painting was disfigured by the poor restoration made by Veglio, and that in 1825 it was retouched by Sebastiano Santi.

On the plinth supporting the figure of a Sibyl, on the right are the Vecellio coat of arms; leaning against it, is a small votive plaque showing Titian and his son Orazio in prayer before a scene of the *Pietà* which is now indistinct.

Plate 40

PIETÀ, *detail of the Magdalene, Venice, Academy.*

" Because all earthly things come to an end, and our life is like a sun setting in the west to rise no more, so Titian, struck by infection, and all paths being closed to him, could not regain his native land and so had to endure the common fate. Thus... he reached his journey's end, felled by the plague in 1576; and though burial rites were barred to all, the authorities bestowed on him the greatest funerary honors; and with a knight's insignia he was buried at the foot of the Altar of the Crucifixion in the Church of the Frari, as in his life he had desired... " (Ridolfi, 1648).

Therefore, we may look upon the *Pietà* as one of the great painter's sublime and most touching achievements through which he wished to be remembered by future generations. And it would require no more than this image of the Magdalene who cries out her grief to the world with the vehemence of a tragic fury to make Titian live through the ages. " May his name never be extinguished, in defiance of Fate which cut his life's thread, and of Time, destroyer of all worldly memory " (Ridolfi).

LIST OF TEXT ILLUSTRATIONS

DRAWINGS

LIST OF COLOR PLATES

THE BLACK AND WHITE ILLUSTRATIONS, COLOR
PLATES, AND TEXT WERE PRINTED AND THE
BOOK BOUND AT THE STABILIMENTO D'ARTI
GRAFICHE OF AMILCARE PIZZI S.p.A., MILAN.